Cyrille Regis MBE

The Matches, Goals, Triumphs and Disappointments

Tony Matthews

First published in 2018 by
Apex Publishing Ltd
www.apexpublishing.co.uk

Print edition typography and formatting by
Andrews UK Limited
www.andrewsuk.com

Contents

About the Author

Tony Matthews was born in West Bromwich during World War II and was an amateur footballer with West Bromwich Albion before playing as a semi-professional in Switzerland. He also had trials with Cliftonville (Ireland), Coventry City (under manager Jimmy Hill), St Johnstone, Walsall and Shrewsbury Town.

Tony has served in the Birmingham Police Force, was a sports master for 10 years and ran a football programme shop in Handsworth (within walking distance of The Hawthorns). From the late 1960s until 2002, he was the official statistician and historian of West Bromwich Albion FC, opening the club's first museum at The Hawthorns in 1995. Tony's personal collection of one million football programmes, including a copy of virtually every one produced by the Albion from the early 1900s, resides in the club's archives, along with some 8,000 Baggies' photographs, cigarette cards and trade cards, also collected by Tony.

Player/manager of the West Bromwich Albion Old Stars (1979-89) Tony also organised hundreds of quizzes over the last 35 years, raising more than £125,000 for various charities. He has also completed two marathons.

Tony has written numerous books on football, the first of which, *Albion at War*, was published in 1976. This second book about Cyrille's career is the 120th book compiled by Tony himself, although he has been involved in the production of a total of 150 books. Over the last 40 years, Tony has covered 25 different clubs, in one form or another, and has written about several top names in the game, including José Mourinho, Steven Gerrard,

Alan Shearer, Ryan Giggs and Ronnie Allen, the former WBA and England centre-forward (who managed the Baggies and other several other clubs).

Tony lives in Spain where he is the sports correspondent for Spectrum FM, an English-speaking radio station, a columnist for two English-produced Spanish newspapers and a charity quiz organiser. He also contributes to the Black County Bugle, a weekly paper, produced in the West Midlands.

Foreword by Ron Atkinson

A player with Oxford United (1960-71) who later managed Cyrille at The Hawthorns (1978-81) and Villa Park (1991-93) as well as being in charge of Cambridge United, Manchester United, Atletico Madrid, Sheffield Wednesday, Coventry City and Nottingham Forest.

I used to tell Cyrille to go out and excite me, and he did just that. I reckoned he was one of the best strikers in world football in the late 1970s. He was big, powerful, thrusting and brave – the sort of fellow who could succeed at almost any sport he chose.

I encouraged him to use these assets to the full. He was quite superb at times and scored some stunning goals, some of them absolute beauties, and they came against some of the top goalkeepers and defenders in the game.

I clearly remember the one he scored against Everton at The Hawthorns, soon after Albion had lost to Ipswich Town in the 1978 FA Cup semi-final. That evening, defender Mick Lyons got hold of Cyrille near the halfway line, rugby-style if you like. But he simply couldn't stop him and, in fact, the Everton centre-half was dragged 40-50 yards downfield by Cyrille who then struck a low shot past George Wood. Soon afterwards, Cyrille scored an even better goal! He controlled Ally Robertson's chipped pass on his chest and when the ball came down, in one sweeping movement, he turned, beat his marker and unleashed a stunning volley that screamed into the top corner of the Everton net before 'keeper Wood could move.

Of the many other brilliant goals he scored when I was his boss, I must choose these from 1978…for Albion in the away League game at Norwich and also in the home FA Cup-tie against the Canaries; against Newcastle at The Hawthorns; away at Manchester City (when he bemused Mick Doyle and Dave Watson); one versus Southampton in a Tennent-Caledonian Cup-tie; against Middlesbrough at home and his cracker in that wonderful 5-3 win at Old Trafford. He then followed up with exceptionally fine strikes against Southampton (away) in 1979, at Crystal Palace in 1980 and versus Sunderland (home) in 1981… and believe you me there were a few more for sure. And during my reign as boss of Villa, he again obliged with some fine efforts, including one on his debut at Sheffield Wednesday and another against one of his favourite teams, Everton. But I knew that each and every goal Cyrille scored was special to him.

Deep down I wish I could have had him with me at Manchester United. It was not to be as I had already secured the services of Bryan Robson and Remi Moses and, realistically, Albion were not likely to welcome any more overtures from Old Trafford in the months that followed.

Of the all the black players I knew and worked with, Cyrille for me was the guv'nor. There's no doubting this and he was certainly up near the top of the list with regards to the best players I ever managed. He was also a genuinely nice guy.

Foreword by Darren Moore

Former Torquay United, Doncaster Rovers, Bradford City, Portsmouth, West Bromwich Albion, Derby County, Barnsley, Burton Albion and Jamaican international defender who made almost 700 club appearances (599 at League level) in 22 years as a professional: 1990-2012. He was appointed caretaker-manager of Albion in early April 2018, and upgraded to full-time manager six weeks later.

In the early eighties, when I was just nine-years-old, my dad sat me down and showed me my first football match on TV. It featured West Bromwich Albion who were in the top flight at the time and Cyrille was playing.

Obviously, as a West Indian, my dad was proud and it was at that point I had the desire to play the professional game myself.

So who would have thought the very man (Cyrille) I watched all those years ago, is the same footballer this foreword has been written about! Amazing! Indeed, it was a great pleasure to be asked by Tony to write a few words about Cyrille – 'Smokin' Joe' – for this wonderful and impressive book which I'm sure everyone who reads it will find encouraging and relate to it in their lives in some way.

I knew Cyrille for a good many years now; we developed a close relationship from when I first got to know him personally when I played against him twice in the 1995-96 season when he was a striker with Chester City and I was a defender with Doncaster Rovers.

I remember looking forward to that first game…I was set to come face to face with a great footballer, a great man, a legend in the professional game, and a player who had struck fear in the minds of some very experienced and international-class defenders during his professional career.

Cyrille was approaching the end of his playing days at the time. He was 37 years of age, yet even then he was a formidable striker and I must admit he gave me a tough time all afternoon although we did win the game 3-0.

In the return game, Cyrille played for an hour or so and I can tell you I was happy when he went off. I had been tested to the limit once again and, on this occasion, he helped Chester gain revenge with a 2-1 victory.

Cyrille, to me, was a great man, a wonderful friend, a mentor and someone from whom I sought great encouragement about the professional game. He helped me develop and understand more and more about football as time passed by.

I could sit down and talk with Cyrille all day, every day. His knowledge of the game was so vast in many areas and in life in general. It was a pleasure to be his friend and to see him play and then go out and compete against him on the football pitch.

For me and for many other black footballers, Cyrille helped open doors and paved the way for our success in the professional game. He was a top man, a great man. Blessings, my friend. R.I.P.

Foreword by Derek Statham

Former West Bromwich Albion, Southampton, Stoke City and Walsall left-back who, between 1976 and 1993, made 535 senior club appearances (15 goals scored) and gained six U21 and three full caps for England.

Cyrille was a great player, and also a great friend. Soon after arriving at West Brom from non-League football, he joined us for pre-season training. He was a big, muscular centre-forward and played in a friendly against Walsall at the training ground. We, the first team squad, had just finished the morning session, so we sat and watched for a few minutes.

Robbie Dennison went down the left wing, crossed to the far post, and 'Cy' climbed above everybody, and thundered a header into the top corner of the net. We all just looked at each other gob-smacked! "Who's that? He looks huge – he's awesome," said skipper John Wile and I totally agreed with JW.

It was our first experience of Cyrille's power and strength. And, needless to say, it didn't take long for him to be amongst us, and be part and parcel of the first team. He went on, of course, to give us and the fans some great memories in the blue and white stripes.

I was sorry to see him move on, but later I did have the pleasure of playing against him as well, as he went on to give outstanding service to all of the other clubs he served throughout a fine career.

He remained a truly great friend to me and my family, and we got together whenever we could.

There is no doubt whatsoever that 'Cy' was a terrific player. He will be sadly missed. R.I.P.

Acknowledgements

I would like to thank, first and foremost, my old pals, the late Bill Goulden (formerly of Peerless Press Printers in West Bromwich) and Laurie Rampling (the West Bromwich Albion lensman) for supplying some terrific photographs of Cyrille Regis.

Also I say thank you sincerely to the following for the information they have supplied, and for checking and re-checking the text including the various stats and facts: my good friends Jim Brown (covering Coventry City), Rob Bishop (Aston Villa's programme editor) and the late John 'Fozzie' Hendley (the media man at Wolverhampton Wanderers); to Daniel Burns and Chas Sumner (for supplying statistics appertaining to Chester City); to John Taylor (likewise of Wycombe Wanderers, who is the official secretary of the club's ex-Players' Association) and to ardent Baggies' fans David Morgan (Bobbo50), Dean Walton, Mark Thomas (Albiontillwedie), Mark 'Snarka' Whitehouse and Roy Morley; to picture-snapper extraordinaire Paul Dennis (Maidstone, Kent); to supporters David Foster (London), Ron Ferriday (Surrey), Gordon Johnstone (Bromley, Kent), Sam Beasley (Birmingham), Geoff Lessington (Chester) and Leslie Thomson (Middlesex) for their assistance; to expert photographer Dave Bagnall (Wolves); to cartoonist Bob Bond; to several members of the former AFS (far too many to list individually); to Li-Wen Pu-Feng (China Xinhua News); to big Ron Atkinson and my two buddies and former Albion players Darren 'Big Dave' Moore and Derek Statham for penning the forewords and to everyone at Apex Publishing for all their valuable input.

Last, but by no means least, I have to say thanks yet again to my 'understanding' and loving wife Margaret for continually putting up with the noise and tediousness of my constant finger-tapping on the computer keyboard…it won't go on forever…just a half-dozen more books to complete before I (and we) can take a well-deserved rest!

This book is dedicated to a truly great footballer
and a very good friend, Cyrille Regis, pioneer,
master goalscorer and legend in his own right.

Choosing Cyrille's Best Matches

How does one even consider selecting the best matches out of the 750+ Cyrille played in at senior level for club and country over a period of 20 years? With great difficulty, I can tell you that for nothing.

Choosing 100 would be hard going, but in the end I pulled out 50 which I feel were defining fixtures in the playing career of one of the game's greatest footballers, Cyrille Regis.

At least half of the games feature the club who gave him his big chance in League football – West Bromwich Albion. I've included his debuts for his first five League clubs and England and his last ever game as a professional footballer; his first goal for Albion and his first for his country (England); special wins, some horrible defeats, a few draws; major disappointments plus a few celebratory matches. And I know, full well, I have upset someone, somewhere for not choosing a specific game. It was a pity, really, that the book couldn't have accommodated 100, even 200 fixtures. All I can say is enjoy and reminisce.

TM.

Cyrille Regis

This Was Your Life

Personal Information:

Born: Cyrille Regis

Birth place/date: Maripasoula, French Guiana, 9 February 1958

Died: Edgbaston, Birmingham, 14 January 2018

Education: Ladbroke Grove and Kensal Rose Primary schools and Cardinal Hinsley RC school, Harlesden.

Playing career: Borough of Brent Boys, Ryder Brent Valley (August 1974), Oxford & Kilburn Boys (January 1975), Carmel Hall FC (briefly), Ryder Brent Valley (March 1975), Molesey FC (August 1975), Hayes (semi-professional, July 1976), West Bromwich Albion (£5,000 May 1977), Happy Valley/Hong Kong (guest, July 1980), Coventry City (£300,000, October 1984, player-coach, April 1988), Aston Villa (free transfer, July 1991), Wolverhampton Wanderers (free transfer, August 1993), Wycombe Wanderers (free transfer, August 1994), Chester City (free transfer, May 1995, retired, May 1996).

After retiring: West Bromwich Albion (coach, February 1997-January 2000; acted as joint caretaker-manager with John Gorman, July-August 1999 and again with Allan Evans, March 2000); became a players' agent, initially with First Artist and then with the Stellar Group, working at the outset with his nephew, Jason Roberts, and later with Darren Bent, Ashley Cole and even Gareth Bale.

Appearances and Goals

Here are details of appearances made and goals scored at senior level by Cyrille: 1977 to 1996 inclusive (all substitute appearances included in totals):

Season	League		FA Cup		League Cup		Others		Totals	
	A	G	A	G	A	G	A	G	A	G
West Bromwich Albion										
1977-78	34	10	6	6	2	2	-	-	42	18
1978-79	39	13	6	1	3	-	10	4	58	18
1979-80	26	8	2	1	2	-	-	-	30	9
1980-81	38	14	2	-	7	3	-	-	47	17
1981-82	37	17	5	2	9	6	2	-	53	25
1982-83	26	9	1	-	2	2	-	-	29	11
1983-84	30	10	3	-	3	3	-	-	36	13
1984-85	7	1	-	-	-	-	-	-	7	1
Totals	237	82	25	10	28	16	12	4	302	112
Coventry City										
1984-85	31	5	1	-	-	-	-	-	32	5
1985-86	34	5	1	-	2	5	-	-	37	10
1986-87	40	12	6	2	5	2	-	-	51	16
1987-88	31	10	2	1	3	-	-	-	37	12
1988-89	34	7	1	-	3	-	-	-	38	7
1989-90	34	4	1	-	7	1	1	-	43	5
1990-91	34	4	4	-	5	3	1	-	44	7
Totals	238	47	16	3	24	12	4	-	282	62
Aston Villa										
1991-92	39	11	5	-	2	-	-	-	46	11
1992-93	13	1	2	-	2	-	-	-	17	1
Totals	52	12	7	-	4	-	-	-	63	12

Season	League		FA Cup		League Cup		Others		Totals	
	A	G	A	G	A	G	A	G	A	G
Wolverhampton Wanderers										
1993-94	19	2	3	-	-	-	1	-	23	2
Wycombe Wanderers										
1994-95	35	9	1	-	2	1	-	-	38	10
Chester City										
1995-96	29	7	1	-	3	-	-	-	33	7
Overall	610	159	53	13	61	29	17	4	741	205

NB: Cyrille also scored 27 goals in 40 first team appearances for Molesey in season 1975-76 and 24 in 61 senior appearances for Hayes in season 1976-77.

International Record:
England: 5 full caps
England U21: 6 caps (3 goals)
England 'B': one cap.
England XI: one app.

Club Honours:
Coventry City: FA Cup winner's 1986-87
Aston Villa: Premier League runners-up 1992-93

Individual Awards:
Hayes: Player of the Year: 1976-77
PFA Young Footballer of the Year: 1977-78
FWA Footballer of the Year runner-up: 1982
PFA Player of the Year runner-up: 1981-82
Won 'Goal of the Season': 1981-82
Birmingham Evening Mail Footballer of the Year: 1986-87
Midlands' Soccer Writer's Player of the Year: 1986-87
Awarded the MBE: 2008

Cyrille Regis MBE

The Matches, Goals, Triumphs and Disappointments

Introduction

To a footballing legend

Known simply as 'Smokin Joe', 'the Big Fella' and 'Big C' by the supporters and 'Reggae' by his Baggies' team-mate Brendon Batson, Cyrille Regis spent seven wonderful years with his first senior club, West Bromwich Albion.

A huge favourite with The Hawthorns' fans from the day he made his debut in a 4–0 home League Cup victory over Rotherham United in August 1977. He was on target twice that evening and thereafter found the back of the net on a regular basis, scoring some quite spectacular and breath-taking goals at home and away in all competitions.

Indeed, he created a club record – possibly something unique – by netting on his debut for Albion in five different competitions… in the Football League (v. Middlesbrough); in the FA Cup (v. Blackpool); in the League Cup (v. Rotherham United); in the Tennent-Caledonian Cup semi-final (v. Southampton) and in the Central League (v. Sheffield Wednesday). And he also scored in his first serious 'behind closed doors' practice game as well!

Strong, muscular and aggressive, he possessed a terrific shot (mainly right-footed); his heading ability was top-class and he could leave opponents standing with his devastating speed over 25 to 30 yards. He would often collect the ball around the halfway line and head towards goal, brushing aside his markers with his powerful shoulders before unleashing a cannonball shot.

TV cameras, thankfully, captured several of his classic goals on film... so that we can relive his explosive style in years to come, especially on YouTube.

Cyrille was certainly a snip of a signing from non-League football, spotted by former Albion centre-forward of the fifties, Ronnie Allen, who initially paid some money out of his own pocket to Hayes to bring him to The Hawthorns!

Subsequently capped by England at full, 'B' and U21 levels, Cyrille was voted PFA 'Young Footballer of the Year' in 1978 and, four years later, was runner-up behind the FWA 'Footballer of the Year', Steve Perryman, and also to the PFA 'Player of the Year', Kevin Keegan.

In 1984, having scored 112 goals in 302 senior appearances for Albion, he was transferred to Coventry City (annoyingly as far as thousands of Baggies' fans were concerned) and, three years later, he helped the Sky Blues win the FA Cup, beating Tottenham Hotspur at Wembley.

Soon after collecting his winner's medal, he was voted the *Birmingham Evening Mail's* 'Footballer of the Year' and was chosen as the Midlands Soccer Writer's 'Player of the Year' after his part in Coventry City's FA Cup triumph.

Cyrille went on to score another 62 goals in 282 games for the Sky Blues before going on to claim 12 more in 63 outings for his third Midland club, Aston Villa.

Thereafter, he struck twice in 23 appearances for Albion's Black Country rivals, Wolves, netted 10 times in 38 games for Wycombe Wanderers and bagged seven in 33 matches for his last League club, Chester City.

Having moved to Molineux from Villa Park in the summer of 1993, Cyrille quickly became the first footballer to play 'professionally' for four major Midland League clubs – Albion, Coventry City, Aston Villa and Wolves. And, on 6 May 1995, at the age of 37 years and 86 days, he became the oldest player ever to turn out in a League game for Wycombe against Leyton Orient and he scored to celebrate the occasion.

Cyrille eventually retired from competitive football in the summer of 1996 with an exceptionally fine record of 205 goals in 741 club games, plus three more in 15 encounters for various England teams.

Several other members of the Regis family are, or have been, involved in sport and they include fellow footballers Dave Regis and Jason Roberts, and Dave's son, Daren; GB Olympic athlete John Regis, MBE; and Jason's sister, Jasmine, who is a notable athlete. And for the record, before he joined non-League club Molesey, Cyrille was offered a trial by Chelsea but had to pull out with a hamstring injury!

Cyrille became a born again Christian after a car crash claimed the life of his close friend Laurie Cunningham in 1989. Both players had been involved in a similar crash two years earlier.

The Story of a True Footballing Legend

Cyrille Regis

Cyrille's father Robert, one of 15 children, was born on 6 April 1916 in the small, picturesque port of Canaries on the Caribbean island of St Lucia.

Initially a fisherman, he changed jobs soon after World War Two and became involved in the gold panning industry in French Guiana where, in 1950, at the age of 34, he met 17-year-old Mathilde Gladys Fadaire, who originated from Guadeloupe. The couple chose to settle in Maripasoula and, in February 1958, Cyrille arrived on the scene. And really speaking Cyrille should have been christened Gilbert!

He said, "In French culture, a baby boy is normally given the name of the saint he is born under, followed by the name chosen by your parents with the family name coming next. "However, when the time came for my parents to register my birth, the person chosen to do so simply forgot to add Gilbert to the official birth certificate!"

Cyrille's parents eventually married in 1961 and dad Robert went by boat to the UK in 1962, followed a year later (February 1963) by his mum, Mathilde, brother, Imbert, and Cyrille himself, all sailing on the Cunard liner *Ascania Two* from St Lucia to Southampton.

The Regis family lived initially on the Portobello Road in the Kensington/Chelsea district of West London, before moving to

Kensal Rise, then to Willesden before residing in Stonebridge in the Borough of Brent.

Brought up and educated in Roman Catholic schools, Cyrille gained a creditable seven CSEs.

As a youngster, Cyrille enjoyed athletics, cricket and, of course, football and when he was at Cardinal Hinsley School, he was called up to represent the Borough of Brent boys' football team. Around this time he also played for a local church team called Carmel Hall.

After starring in the Sunday League for Ryder Brent Valley, he switched to Oxford and Kilburn youth club (known as the OK club) before rejoining Ryder Brent Valley. And, around this time, he was also offered a trial by Chelsea but was unable to take advantage due to injury and was asked if he would like to attend training sessions by Tottenham Hotspur.

Cyrille recalled, "Unfortunately, I couldn't attend classes in the afternoon and it was a bit of a rush to get to the training ground in the evenings, so I declined the offer."

On leaving school, Cyrille chose to be an electrician, eventually gaining a City and Guilds diploma. He continued to practice this trade until moving into professional football... just in case something occurred and he was forced to quit the game. "You never know what can happen in life," he said.

Moving into the world of football in the summer of 1975, Cyrille signed for the Athenian League club Molesey for whom he scored 26 goals during his only season with the club. He was then approached by Boreham Wood FC but elected not to sign for his local rivals. However, Cyrille later discovered that he was too young to be under a professional contract and quit Molesey to join the semi-professional side Hayes of the Isthmian League, officially signing on 7 July 1976.

Cyrille struck 24 goals for Hayes in the 1976–77 season during which time he had been watched by the Millwall manager, Gordon

Jago, and Charlie Hurley, boss of Reading, as well as by West Bromwich Albion's chief scout, Ronnie Allen, who recommended to his manager (Johnny Giles), chairman (Bert Millichip) and the club's board of directors, that Albion should sign him quickly!

Allen had gone along to an evening Isthmian League game to watch Cyrille in action. It was freezing cold, the pitch was bone hard and bumpy but he was mightily impressed with what he saw! After 10 minutes, Hayes won a corner and when the ball came over, despite being well marked, Cyrille rose majestically to power home a thumping header, the ball and three defenders going into the net all at the same time. Said Allen, "Yes – that'll do for me – he's my man."

However, certain directors were undecided – unsure in fact – about splashing out a four-figure fee for such a young, unproven player. Allen offered to fund any initial payment from his own pocket, so sure was he that Cyrille would do the business (score goals that is) in the top Division of English football.

The Albion board had second thoughts in the end, without Allen putting in any of his own money – although he was still willing to do so – the transfer duly went ahead in May 1977, when a fee of £5,000 was paid to Hayes, with another £5,000 following after Cyrille had made 20 senior appearances. In fact, his boss at Hayes, Bobby Ross, told Allen, "Cyrille's got wings – let him fly!"

It transpired that Giles said that he would not sign any players unless he had seen them in action for himself.

By coincidence, soon after Cyrille's arrival at The Hawthorns, Allen took over as team manager, following the resignation of the former Leeds midfielder Giles.

And as mentioned earlier, Cyrille made a terrific start to his Baggies' career.

After his double-debut strike against Rotherham United in the League Cup, the goals continued to fly in, left right and centre, against a variety of opponents.

The one he netted in his first League game was described by Middlesbrough's David Mills, who later became a team-mate of Cyrille's at Albion, as 'a goal of sheer brilliance'… and he had already scored a few beauties himself.

Initially, Cyrille teamed up with another black player at The Hawthorns – Laurie Cunningham – who had been signed from Leyton Orient for £110,000, in March 1977. After Ron Atkinson had taken over as manager from Allen, another black player, Brendon Batson, joined the clan from 'Big Ron's' former employers, Cambridge United.

At this time, it was very unusual for an English football club to simultaneously field three black players together in the same first team… although Albion's trio were not, by any means, the first black footballers to play professionally in England.

Affectionately called 'The Three Degrees' (a slogan name chosen by Atkinson after the famous American vocal trio of the same name), Messrs Batson, Cunningham and Regis became an integral part of Albion's first team.

In the summer of 1978, Cyrille was given the chance to join French club St. Etienne. A French lawyer, Christian Durancie, got in touch with Cyrille and arranged a meeting with officials of St. Etienne. It transpired that a fee of £750,000 had been placed on Albion's table. If the deal went through Cyrille's wages would increase from £60 a week to £500 a week!

Head coach of St Etienne, Robert Herbin, had earlier come over to watch Cyrille score twice in Albion's 3-1 win over Everton in the April, and it must be said was 'mightily impressed'.

Atkinson never wanted Cyrille to leave Albion, describing him as 'Black Gold'… "No way am I going to lose him," he said.

As it happened, the transfer never happened… after Cyrille was told that if he moved to France, the likelihood was that he could be conscripted into the French Army. He was happy to stay at The Hawthorns and to continue playing with his best pal, Laurie

Cunningham, who, in a year's time, would leave Albion and join Real Madrid for almost a million pound.

In the meantime, Albion duly increased Cyrille's wages from £60 a week to £200 a week.

"That was a considerable rise in anyone's language… and the gaffer also offered me £2,500 to sign a new contract with Albion. I did just that," said Cyrille. "I was over the moon."

Cyrille, who at the time was being pen-pictured in all programmes and football magazines as being a strong, powerful centre-forward, blessed with speed, great heading ability and booming shot – was voted PFA 'Young Player of the Year' in 1978 and, four years later, his cracking strike against Norwich City in an FA Cup-tie, was chosen as *Match of the Day*'s 'Goal of the Season'.

Unfortunately, Cyrille did not manage to win a major honour at The Hawthorns. Albion were defeated in two FA Cup semi-finals, first by Ipswich Town in 1978 and then by Queens Park Rangers four years later, both games being played at Highbury. The Baggies were also ousted in the quarter-finals of the UEFA Cup by Red Star Belgrade in 1979, lost a two-legged League Cup semi-final against Tottenham Hotspur in 1982 and finished third in the First Division in 1979 and fourth in 1981.

In May 1982, Cyrille was sent off for the first time in his career by referee Brian Stevens – for a landing a 75th minute right hook on the Aston Villa defender, and future Albion man, Ken McNaught. "He was at me all through the game – I lost my rag and hit him. He made the most of it anyway," said Cyrille.

Albion lost the game 1-0, Pat Heard scoring with 90 seconds remaining.

Cyrille finally scored against Villa for the first time in a 4-3 opening day League defeat in August 1983 but later in the season Albion gained sweet revenge with a 3-1 home victory, courtesy of a brace from Garry Thompson and a smart effort by Cyrille.

A year or so later, in September 1984, Cyrille received his second red card, this time in a League game at Sunderland… for lashing out at Shaun Elliott, having earlier been cautioned. Again, he was frustrated by the robust and foul tackling. The game ended in a 1-1 draw.

Soon after serving his suspension, and playing his last game for Albion against Manchester United at The Hawthorns, former Baggies' player and future manager Bobby Gould signed Cyrille for Coventry City for £250,000 + VAT. Gould said, "This is a snip-of-a-signing for the club."

Recalled Cyrille, "I had lost my spark and I needed to get my game going again and that's why I joined Coventry." Ironically though, manager Gould left Highfield Road six weeks after signing Cyrille – replaced by Don Mackay.

Cyrille went on to spend seven decent seasons at Highfield Road, forming useful strike partnerships with Terry Gibson, Keith Houchen, Kevin Gallacher, fiery Scot David Speedie and briefly with Steve Livingstone. And it was his goals that effectively kept the Sky Blues in the top flight in 1985.

Two years later, under manager George Curtis and head coach John Sillett, he helped Coventry win the FA Cup, enjoying his best season since his heyday at The Hawthorns in the process as the team, at last, tactically began to play to his strengths.

Cyrille was certainly a key member of the Sky Blues' Cup winning team in 1987, scoring arguably one of his finest ever goals for the Sky Blues in a quarter-final victory over Sheffield Wednesday.

He also helped Coventry reach the 1990 League Cup semi-final, when they were beaten over two legs by Nottingham Forest. And he was in the Sky Blues' team that lost to non-Leaguers Sutton United in the 3rd round of the FA Cup in January 1988.

"That was a bit of a shocker," said Cyrille, "We never expected that. It was a catastrophic moment. I had played at Sutton's ground, Gander Green Lane, when I was with Hayes, so I knew what to expect.

"Sutton, although based in mid-table of the GM Vauxhall Conference, were no mugs, and their muddy pitch was a great leveller. It was horrible. They raised their game and brought us down to their level. It was a humiliating defeat."

Cyrille's form with Coventry also earned him a recall to the England team in 1987. Selected to play against Turkey in a European Championship qualifier at Wembley in October 1987, he came on as a second-half substitute for Peter Beardsley.

At the time he was only the third Coventry player to win a full England cap – after goalkeeper Reg Matthews in 1956 and full-back Danny Thomas in 1982.

Cyrille had the pleasure of scoring in the Sky Blues' first ever League win over his future club, Aston Villa, in November 1988 and also became the first Sky Blues' player to net a winning goal at Anfield, doing so a year later.

Whilst his infrequent strike rate provoked criticism among Coventry supporters, he always gave 100 per cent and when he did find the net, his goal was often something special.

Perhaps the most fitting summary of his time at Highfield Road should be a statistical one, in that only Dion Dublin has surpassed Cyrille's goalscoring record for the Sky Blues in the modern game.

Following Sillett's departure in November 1990, and the raft of changes made under new boss, Terry Butcher, Cyrille was sold to Aston Villa in the summer of 1991, at the age of 33, being reunited with his former Albion manager Ron Atkinson.

Boss man Butcher declined to offer Cyrille a new contract, so he left Highfield Road on a free transfer.

Partnering Dalian Atkinson in the Villa attack, Cyrille, to a certain degree, rediscovered his goal-scoring touch, finishing the 1991-92 campaign with 11 goals. However, in 1992-93 his first team chances were somewhat limited following the arrival of

Dean Saunders, but Villa, nevertheless, finished runners-up in the first Premier League season, beaten to the title by another of the manager's former clubs, Manchester United.

One thing Cyrille remembers during his time at Villa Park is that manager Ron Atkinson had no less than 10 black players in his first team squad in 1992-93 – Dalian Atkinson, Earl Barrett, Mark Blake, Martin Carruthers, Tony Daley, Ugo Ehiogu (ex-West Bromwich Albion), Paul McGrath, Bryan Small, Dwight Yorke and, of course, Cyrille himself.

Cyrille subsequently joined his fourth Midlands club in 1993, moving back into the Black Country with Albion's arch-rivals Wolverhampton Wanderers, signed by manager Graham Turner.

However, once again his first-team opportunities were restricted due to the form of fellow strikers Steve Bull (another ex-Baggie) and David Kelly, meaning that Cyrille made just eight League starts in his only season at Molineux. And, when former England boss Graham Taylor replaced Turner in the Wolves' hot seat, he quickly off-loaded Cyrille to Wycombe Wanderers of Division One.

Twelve months later, Cyrille was off again – this time to Division Two side Chester City. He did okay for a while with the lower League club and, after striking up an excellent rapport with the fans, he played his last game at competitive level in February 1996, starring in a 2-1 win away at Doncaster Rovers.

Cyrille duly announced his retirement as a player playing in October 1996, at the age of 38 – this after failing to recover fully from an injury sustained in his final outing for Chester.

And finally I have to say that as a player, Cyrille endured unspeakable abuse in order to ease the way for others. After braving racist remarks, horrible monkey chants, boos and flying bananas, he became a significant role model for succeeding generations of young black players. He was a pioneer to black footballers all over the world.

International Career

Cyrille's dual French and British nationality made him eligible to play internationally for either France or England. He chose the latter and went on to win five full, six U21 and three 'B' caps as well as playing for an England XI.

He made his U21 debut in September 1978, in Denmark; gained his first 'B' cap against Czechoslovakia in Prague two months later and won his first full cap in February 1982 at Wembley.

Cyrille's other two games for the 'B' team came in 1980, against the USA and Australia.

He scored his first goal in an England shirt, in a 3-1 U21 international away win over Bulgaria in June 1979 – a result that helped England reach the latter stages of the 1980 European Championship, although it was the only one out of six qualifying matches in which Cyrille participated.

He played in the away legs of both the quarter-final and semi-final, when England lost to East Germany. His other U21 goals were scored against Sweden in 1979 and Denmark in another ECQ in 1982.

Despite winning five senior caps, Cyrille never played the full 90 minutes for his country, coming on as a substitute on three occasions while twice being substituted himself.

He made his international debut in February 1982, in a 4–0 home win over Northern Ireland in the Home International Championship – replacing Trevor Francis in the 65th minute. In fact, when the players crossed on the touchline, Francis tapped Cyrille on the shoulder and said, "Enjoy it – it's your big day."

Prior to Cyrille, the last Albion striker to be capped was Jeff Astle v. Czechoslovakia in the World Cup in Mexico in 1970.

Unfortunately, Cyrille missed the 1982 World Cup finals with a tedious hamstring injury. Francis, Kevin Keegan Paul Mariner, Peter Withe and Tony Woodcock were the forwards chosen by manager Ron Greenwood who nevertheless named Cyrille as a stand-by reserve with Tony Morley. No consolation really!

Cyrille's final international appearance was in October 1987 when he came on for the last 20 minutes of England's 8-0 demolition of Turkey 8-0 at Wembley. He was the third black player to be capped by England at the highest level – following Viv Anderson and his former Albion team-mate, Laurie Cunningham.

After Football

After retiring as a player, Cyrille was engaged in a variety of coaching roles. Indeed, he returned in that role with Albion in 1997 to look after the reserve side, and twice acted as the Baggies' caretaker-manager before becoming an accredited football agent, initially with First Artist, situated at Wembley and managed by Phil and John Smith. He spent two years with that company before teaming up with the Stellar Group, representing their Midland-based players.

Cyrille was awarded an honorary fellowship by the University of Wolverhampton in 2001 and, three years later, in 2004, was voted as West Bromwich Albion's all-time Cult Hero in a BBC Sport poll, gaining 65% of the vote.

In the same year he was named as one of Albion's 16 greatest-ever players, in a poll organised as part of the club's 125th anniversary celebrations. And he was proud to be asked to be an ambassador for England's 2018 World Cup bid.

Cyrille is also honorary president of the Midland Junior Premier Football League, which caters for players aged between 12 and 18, under the youth development scheme.

Cyrille and his second wife, Julia, visited water-related projects in Ethiopia in 2007, as part of their continued support for WaterAid.

He also won the Coventry City London Supporters' Club Player of the Year in 1987 and regularly comes in high in any Sky Blue legend polls. In 2008, a Coventry City Hall of Fame picture gallery was erected at the club's Ricoh Arena containing 30 all-time

Coventry greats since the war, among them was the man himself, Cyrille Regis.

He was presented with the Member of the Order of the British Empire (MBE) in the Queen's Birthday Honours list of 2008. This was awarded to him for services to the voluntary sector and football. Sadly, by this time, Cyrille's father (in December 1999) and his mother (in January 2000) had both passed away. He just wished they had been alive to see him shake hands with the Queen.

The Regis Family in Sport

Cyrille's brother, Dave, was a professional footballer, serving with Barnet, Notts County, Plymouth Argyle, AFC Bournemouth, Leyton Orient, Lincoln City, Stoke City, Birmingham City, Southend United, Barnsley, Peterborough United and Scunthorpe United in that order between 1988 and 1998, scoring 64 goals in 259 League and Cup games.

And now Dave's son, Daren, has already gained England U18 honours as a forward.

Cyrille was also the uncle of another footballer, Jason Roberts, MBE, ex-Hayes, Wolverhampton Wanderers (reserves), Torquay United, Bristol City, Bristol Rovers, West Bromwich Albion, Portsmouth, Wigan Athletic, Blackburn Rovers and Reading. He scored 168 goals in 509 games between 1995 and 2015 and also played international football for Grenada. Cyrille himself acted as Jason's agent.

Cyrille was the cousin of British Olympic athletic John Regis. His half-brother is Otis Roberts, who played football in Grenada and gained international recognition, while his niece, Yasmin Regis, has competed at the triple jump, and stepson, Marshall (from Cyrille's wife Julia's first marriage) is a talented professional dancer in London.

Fifty Defining Fixtures

There is no better place to start than right at the beginning with Cyrille's first competitive game... his senior debut as a professional footballer for West Bromwich Albion.

1: Football League Cup, 2ⁿᵈ Round

WEST BROMWICH ALBION 4 ROTHERHAM UNITED 0

31 August 1977

Albion, managed by Ronnie Allen, had been dumped out of the League Cup by teams from a lower division in each of the previous four seasons, losing, in turn, to Exeter City, Norwich City, Fulham and Brighton. They didn't want a repeat prescription against Rotherham, who at the time of visiting The Hawthorns, were lying 12ᵗʰ in the Third Division, having already been involved in two League games with score lines of 3-2 (won one, lost one) as well as having to battle through three games and a penalty shoot-out, before knocking out York City in the first round of the League Cup.

However, the Yorkshire club's manager, Jimmy McGuigan, was optimistic about his side's chances against Albion, saying: "Let's wait and see."

In their three League games at the start of the season Albion had beaten Chelsea 3-0 at home, drew 2-2 at Leeds and lost 3-0 to Liverpool at Anfield. The team had been unchanged in each of these games with David Cross leading the line. But he was ruled out against Rotherham, as was Tony Brown, and that left the door open for new signing Cyrille Regis to make his senior debut.

The striker had already found the net in a training ground friendly against Walsall, made a goal for Ally Brown and scored himself in the 22ⁿᵈ minute of his second XI debut against Sheffield Wednesday and was 'as keen as mustard' to see what he could do at first team level. And his manager had no hesitation in naming him as Cross's replacement, telling him: "Go out and do your best."

Cyrille recalled: "I found out I was playing just after training had finished on the morning of the game. With Tony Brown, 'Crossy' and Ally Brown all out injured, I knew I had a chance of being in the team, but when the boss told me to go home and get some rest, because you are playing tonight, I was still gobsmacked, but also happy. I knew the manager had faith in me and that meant a lot."

*Some 33 years earlier, in January 1954, Albion had beaten Rotherham United 4-0 in a home 4*th *round FA Cup-tie. And they had also defeated the Millers 4-0 in a friendly at Millmoor in July 1969.*

WBA: Godden; Mulligan (Trewick), Statham, Martin, Wile, Robertson, Cantello, Cunningham, Regis, Robson, Johnston.

Rotherham United: McAlister; Forrest, Brecken, Rhodes, Stancliffe, Spencer, Finney, Phillips, Gwyther, Goodfellow, Crawford.

Attendance: 15,005

Prior to this Cup game at The Hawthorns, Cyrille had only played before crowds of barely 500… he was now set to face 15,000 spectators under floodlights and inside a pretty big stadium. "I was nervous I can tell you that," he said.

Pushed up front with two of the game's quickest players – Laurie Cunningham to his right and Willie Johnston on the left-wing – Cyrille said: 'I ran round like a headless chicken during the first five or 10 minutes. There were no tactics, I just followed my instincts.'

Cyrille had a couple of decent chances during the first-half which Albion dominated, allowing Rotherham very little time or space in which to play. Indeed, one passing sequence involving five Albion players lasted for almost four minutes, with over 40 passes being completed.

Albion led 2-0 at the interval with goals from centre-half John Wile on seven minutes (although his effort took a slight deflection off Tom Spencer) and an exquisite 25-yarder from Irish Tinkerman Mick Martin just before the half hour mark.

In fact, several newspaper reports list the unfortunate Spencer as the scorer of Albion's first goal but Albion, after consultation, credited it to their skipper – and why not? This was his first in the League Cup for the Baggies and only one more followed, versus Coventry City in September 1979.

Rotherham's only meaningful efforts before half-time came from ex-Swansea City striker David Gwyther and winger Richard Finney.

Encouraged by his colleagues in the dressing room and by the Hawthorns' faithful in the stands, Cyrille went out after the break all revved up and he responded in terrific style. Every touch of the ball was greeted by loud cheering. There were no boos, jeers, groans or moans, just encouragement, not only from the fans, but from his team-mates as well.

With Albion well in control, they were awarded a penalty in the 60th minute and immediately the crowd shouted out 'Ceer-ul, Ceer-ul'… demanding that he should step up and take the spot kick.

In 'Bomber' Brown's absence, Willie Johnston had been given the job of penalty-taker, but after consulting with Len Cantello, the Scot waved his hand in the direction of Cyrille and said, "Go on then, you have a go."

Cyrille had never before taken a penalty (at any level) but, facing the Brummie Road faithful, he ran up confidently, head down and cracked the ball hard and high past goalkeeper Tom McAlister and into the net at the Smethwick End of the ground. The crowd roared; the tension eased considerably; Cyrille had scored his first senior goal for Albion… 111 were to follow in due course.

Indeed, his second came in the 74th minute and what a beauty it was too. A quick passing movement took Albion down the Rotherham left and, from Cunningham's teasing cross, Cyrille chested the ball down ran on and cracked it home right-footed from a tight angle. The Baggies' supporters went wild – they had found a new hero. Four nil, game over… what a start for Cyrille.

One reporter wrote: 'Johnston had the wings to himself… Cantello dominated midfield… and Regis, Cunningham and Co. cruised through the game up front… but my 'Man of the Match' was Derek Statham – he was brilliant. Cyrille ran him a close second!'

After the match, it was learned that manager Allen had torn a strip off Johnston for allowing Cyrille to take the penalty. "If he had missed and Rotherham had gone up the other end and scored, we would have had to fight to hold on for a win," said Allen.

On leaving the ground, Cyrille, along with a four of his team-mates, joined supporters across the road in The Hawthorns Hotel for a celebratory drink. It was after 3am when some finally got home!

I know, I was there. Thankfully, Albion were given a day off from training that morning!

Tony Brown sat in the Halfords Lane stand to witness Cyrille's superb debut. He said, in so many words, "Cyrille looked very raw when I first saw him, but after scoring that stunning goal, that was it. The fans went crackers. He was their favourite!"

And it was the *Express & Star* newspaper that carried this headline, and appropriately so: 'Nice One Cyrille'.

2: Football League Division One

WEST BROMWICH ALBION 2 MIDDLESBROUGH 1

3 September 1977

After his two-goal debut against Rotherham United, Cyrille's name was in the headlines of virtually every newspaper – in the Midland-based ones especially – with 'King Regis is Debut Demon' and 'The New Astle' just two of them. Cyrille, himself, thought: 'I like this, it feels good' but he was not sure if he would be chosen to play in his first League game against Middlesbrough.

Manager Ronnie Allen said: "I dare not leave him out on Saturday because the crowd will have my head." That was it. Cyrille retained his position and was set to make his First Division debut at the age of 19 and a half. With Tony Brown side-lined and Mick Martin injured, John Trewick came into the team for the only change from that which had knocked Rotherham out of the League Cup.

Middlesbrough, managed by the former Aston Villa full-back John Neal, had beaten near neighbours Newcastle United 2-0 in their previous League game, having started the campaign with 1-1 draws against Liverpool and Norwich City. They had also held Sunderland to a 2-2 draw in the League Cup. In their attack, the Teesiders had David Mills who, in January 1979, would become Britain's first £500,000 footballer when he moved from Ayresome Park to The Hawthorns. But hard-tackling midfielder Graeme Souness was missing.

At the time of kick-off Albion were lying 12th in the table with Middlesbrough eighth.

WBA: Godden; Mulligan, Statham, Trewick (W. Hughes), Martin, Wile, Robertson, Cantello, Cunningham, Regis, Robson, Johnston.

Middlesbrough: Platt; Craggs, Cooper, Boam, Maddren, Brine, Mahoney, Mills, Ashcroft, McAndrew, Armstrong.

Attendance: 19,044

Albion began brightly with Cyrille setting up half-chances for both Cunningham and Robson while Boro's robust defender Stuart Boam almost diverted Paddy Mulligan's deceptive free-kick past his own 'keeper.

Albion deservedly took the lead in the 17th minute. Derek Statham found space on the left and from his high, looping cross John Wile headed the ball back towards the centre of the penalty area towards Cyrille. His shot was blocked but the ball broke free to Robson who smashed hard and low through a crowd of players and into Jim Platt's net.

Four minutes later it was 2-0… with Cyrille scoring a quite stunning and memorable goal. Collecting a loose ball 10 yards inside his own half of the field, he evaded a lunging tackle from Boam, chested the ball down, turned round and took off… beating three defenders and breezing past a fourth before steering his shot wide of Platt. It was some goal. The whole ground erupted to celebrate a remarkable individual effort, with chants of 'Astle is back, Astle is back' ringing round the stands. Even the 'The King' himself hadn't scored a goal like this.

Middlesbrough were being outplayed and Albion could well have increased their lead before half-time, Cyrille and Johnston both going close. Mills tried his best for the visitors, but their only worthwhile effort on goal prior to the interval came from John Mahoney, whose 43rd minute effort was comfortably gathered by Tony Godden.

After the break it was a slightly different story and with Albion's defensive still digesting their cuppas, Mahoney created an opening for Mills who reduced the deficit with a well struck shot on 47 minutes.

Cyrille then burst from midfield again and it took four defenders to stop him. Then winger Johnston overran the ball when steaming in on goal while Platt tipped Robson's shot over the crossbar.

Twice in the last quarter of the game Cunningham came close to adding to Albion's tally. The impressive Platt proved the obstacle first time, pulling the save of the game by brilliantly turning the forward's low shot round a post and it was the woodwork which denied Cunningham soon afterwards and, even then, Platt reacted superbly to deny Robson who was quickest to the rebound.

It was a League debut to remember for Cyrille who would, of course, go on and score many more memorable goals after this sensational effort against one of the toughest defences in the League.

In fact, that's why this game is included in my 'Fifty Defining Fixtures'… just because of THAT GOAL – one of the best I, and thousands of others, have ever seen scored at The Hawthorns.

Tony 'Bomber' Brown, again watching from the stand, said: "Cyrille scored a fantastic goal; the way the youngest beat three experienced Middlesbrough defenders so easily – incredible, really, for a lad from the non-League."

Even Albion's manager Allen said after the match: "It was one of the greatest goals ever scored at the Albion – 10 times better than I ever scored. It was a wonder strike and was worth the entrance fee alone."

Cyrille netted another terrific goal in Albion's next game, a 3-0 win at Newcastle, and soon afterwards scored twice in his first Midlands derby, in a 3-1 win over Birmingham City.

3: FA Cup 3rd Round

WEST BROMWICH ALBION 4 BLACKPOOL 1

7 January 1978

The last time Albion had played Blackpool in the FA Cup was in the third round in January 1964. The Baggies won 1-0 in a replay at Bloomfield Road following a 2-2 draw. At the time, Tony Brown was in the reserves while Cyrille was approaching his sixth birthday!

Both would take the field against the Seasiders in this battle, early in 1978, while the visitors had former Albion goalkeeper Bob Ward between the posts. And for Cyrille it was, of course, his debut in the competition as an Albion player.

At the time of this encounter, Albion were lying sixth in the First Division; Blackpool were ninth in Division Two and were being managed by Bob Stoke who, five years earlier, had guided Sunderland to a remarkable 1-0 victory over Leeds United in the 1973 final.

Manager Ronnie Allen had left The Hawthorns for Saudi Arabia on a £100,000 a year contract, just before Christmas and the club put skipper John Wile in charge of the team.

With Ron Atkinson ready to step into The Hawthorns' hot seat on 13 January, 'Wiley' wanted to register a victory to set things up nicely for the new boss.

"We were certainly up for it," said Cyrille. "The dressing room was buzzing and Big John knew that Albion would win."

WBA: Godden; Martin, Statham, T. Brown, Wile, Robertson, Cunningham, Regis, A. Brown, Trewick, Johnston.

Blackpool: Ward; Gardner, Milligan, Ronson, McEwan, Suddaby, Ainscow, Hart, Walsh, Hatton, Groves (Chandler).

Attendance: 21,306

Albion had Mick Martin deputising for Paddy Mulligan at right-back, while Derek Statham returned on the left flank in place of the versatile Bryan Robson, who pulled out with a sore shin an hour before kick-off.

It was Martin who was first on the attack. However, his weak cross was easily dealt with by Ward. The former Wolves and Birmingham City striker Bob Hatton had Blackpool's first effort on goal but his effort lacked power.

With John Wile and Ally Robertson looking solid at the back, and with Albion seemingly in control, they went in front in the fifth minute through Scottish left-winger Willie Johnston, who was already teasing and tormenting his marker, Gardner.

Soon after Johnston's goal – his third in the FA Cup for the Baggies – Tony Brown should have added a second.

Blackpool, though, were no mugs and, in the 22nd minute, they stunned the home crowd by drawing level. Willie Ronson and Paul Hart linked up in midfield, the latter fed Micky Walsh who in turn set up Bob Hatton to score low past Tony Godden.

Before half-time, as Albion again pressed forward, Cyrille had a chance, but miscued with his right foot and Ward saved comfortably from Ally Brown.

After the interval, Albion immediately picked up the pace and Ward had to be at his best to deny both Cyrille and Johnson, while Cunningham and Ally Brown could have done better with half-chances that came their way. Meanwhile, Hatton and England youth international Alan Ainscow tested Godden during a decent spell by the visitors.

In the 54th minute Regis burst onto the scene to make it 2-1. Receiving the ball out wide, he cut inside his marker before unleashing a vicious swerving cross-shot which beat Ward all ends up.

A quarter-of-an-hour later, things got a bit easier for the Baggies when they were awarded a penalty by Barnsley referee Keith Styles after Cyrille had been brought crashing down inside the area by Peter Suddaby.

Step forward 'Bomber' Brown who was hesitant in what to do with his spot kick – blast the ball hard and straight, place it, or drive it low into a corner?

He knew that 'keeper Ward had seen him take numerous penalties in practice when he was at The Hawthorns. Indeed, after the game 'Wardy' said that he expected Tony to smash the ball down the middle of the goal – virtually straight at him in fact.

Believing this, Ward bobbed around on his line, but 'Bomber' ran up and steered the ball directly and precisely, low into the corner of the net as 'Wardy' veered to the other side. And, as the former Albion 'keeper went to retrieve the ball, he muttered to his old buddy, "You b***d."

Albion continued to attack and after Tony Brown had been fouled, the free-kick found its way out to Statham whose cross was headed straight at Ward by John Wile. That should have sewn up victory.

Blackpool were still in the tie and after Walsh had fired into the side-netting, Johnston, who it must be said had a terrific game, netted a fourth with five minutes remaining

Even after that, Cunningham and Cyrille both had chances to add to Albion's goal tally but a lack of concentration allowed Ward to pull off two decent saves.

Unfortunately, the Bloomfield Road club went from bad to worse after this FA Cup exit. They slipped right down the table, eventually tumbling through the trap-door and into the Third Division. And one of their players, left-winger Alan Groves, sadly passed away in June 1978, aged only 29.

By the time Atkinson had moved in, Albion knew who they would be playing in the next round – it was holders Manchester United away. "Oh well," he said, "that's football!"

4: FA Cup 4th Round Replay

WEST BROMWICH ALBION 3 MANCHESTER UNITED 2
(after extra time)

1 February 1978

Having taken charge of his first Albion game (a 1-0 defeat at Middlesbrough) Ron Atkinson's next match as Baggies' boss was a fourth round FA Cup-tie away to the holders Manchester United.

He went to Old Trafford minus Laurie Cunningham (laid low with a stomach bug) and the suspended Ally Robertson whose run of 116 consecutive League appearances had just come to an end.

In miserable wet conditions, and with Bryan Robson playing alongside John Wile at the heart of Albion's defence, Atkinson's team battled it out to earn a 1-1 draw in front of more than 57,000 spectators. Willie Johnston literally 'rolled' the Baggies in front on 76 minutes but with barely a minute remaining, a speculative 25-yard fizzer from Steve Coppell skidded across the mud, hit a post and rebounded into the net off 'keeper Tony Godden's shoulder, to earn United a replay.

After the game Johnston said: "We'll murder 'em at The Hawthorns."

Albion were unchanged for the replay and, before his first home game as manager, Atkinson told his players, "Go out and express yourselves."

Cyrille was certainly up for the challenge, saying: "I am confident we can win this one – and I'm going to score!"

WBA: Godden; Mulligan, Statham, T. Brown, Wile (W. Hughes), Robson, Martin, A. Brown, Regis, Trewick, Johnston.

Manchester United: Roche; Nicholl, Albiston (J. Greenhoff), Buchan, Houston, McIlroy, Coppell, Macari, Jordan, Pearson, Hill.

Attendance: 37,792

On another wet pitch, Albion got off to a terrific start and in the 14th minute, Tony Brown, with a wonderful pass from inside his own half, sent Johnston sprinting away down the United right. The Scottish winger took on, and beat, future Albion defender Jimmy Nicholl before crossing high into the penalty area where Ally Brown rose highest to nod the ball down to his namesake who had raced 50 yards upfield to join the attack. Without hesitation, 'Bomber', from near the penalty spot, let fly with a right-footed shot which flew hard and low past Paddy Roche.

Six minutes later, United equalised when Steve Coppell and Joe Jordan combined to set up Sammy McIlroy, who quickly switched the ball inside for Stuart Pearson (later to become an Albion coach) who scored with a precise right-footed shot, low past Godden's right hand.

Both teams had half-chances before half-time, Cyrille going closest for Albion while Jordan saw a free header saved by Godden.

Four minutes into the second-half, Johnston, in acres of space, collected Mick Martin's astute pass, turned Nicholl inside out (again) and cracked a shot against the United crossbar. Cyrille, reacting quickest, was there to knock the rebound over the line to put Albion back in front.

Soon afterwards, Jordan fractured the jaw of Baggies' skipper Wile with his elbow (no red card!). "This was an awful challenge," said Willie Johnston, an international colleague of Jordan's.

Wile went off and on came 19-year-old Wayne Hughes who was pushed into midfield with Martin dropping back into defence alongside Robson.

Albion immediately came under pressure, and the 'makeshift' defensive pairing played brilliantly, holding off swarms of United attacks. Two tackles by Martin were stupendous.

After Johnston had been booked for crashing into McIlroy, Pearson shot straight at Godden and Gordon Hill fired wide. But the Baggies' defence, bravely and gallantly, withstood the bombardment – until 15 seconds from time when Hill fired in a hopeful shot.

Amazingly, just like the incident at Old Trafford, the ball struck a post, rebounded, hit Godden on the head and fell into the net. One-all – 30 minutes of extra time to play... not what Albion wanted!

This was a body-blow without doubt, but Atkinson went onto the pitch and reassured his players that they were 'better than United' and should go out and win the game. "You've beaten them twice – now go out and do it again," he said.

And what a terrific start they made in extra time. After just 26 seconds, following a throw-in deep in United's half of the field, Tony Brown played a delightful pass through to John Trewick on the right side of the penalty area. 'Tucka' pulled the ball back behind Martin Buchan for Ally Brown, whose effort struck the bar, but Cyrille was in the right place at the right time to send the rebound past Roche and into the net from close range. There was great joy all around The Hawthorns!

United were stunned. They were unable to raise their game and Albion comfortably held out for the next 29 minutes to earn a 5th round tie against Derby County at The Baseball Ground – where they had not won a competitive match since December 1919.

After this win over United, a delighted Atkinson said: "When I go to a match I want to be thrilled and excited by thrustful and attacking football… and Albion did just that."

Cyrille admitted: "It was a great win, a fantastic atmosphere and it got the ball rolling for Ron."

5: FA Cup 6th Round

WEST BROMWICH ALBION 2 NOTTINGHAM FOREST 0

11 March 1978

After beating Derby County at long last by three goals to two – Cyrille netted twice, both headers, and Johnston once – it was Albion against Brian's Clough's Nottingham Forest in a quarter-final tie at The Hawthorns.

In-form Forest, sitting proudly on top of the First Division, were on a 22-game unbeaten run in all games, stretching back 19 November, and were all set to face Liverpool in the League Cup final.

Albion had drawn two and won one of their three League games since beating the Rams, but manager Ron Atkinson was a little concerned about the number of goals being conceded. Paddy Mulligan had missed those matches but Ally Robertson was now back in the team.

The last time Albion had reached the semi-finals of the FA Cup was in 1969 when they lost 1-0 to Leicester City. And they were quietly confident of overcoming Forest and making it into the last four of the prestigious competition for the 18th time in the club's history.

Cyrille had scored in every round so far – a feat achieved by the legendary Jeff Astle in 1968 when the Baggies last won the trophy. Cyrille knew all about this but said in a pre-match press interview: "People are already starting to draw parallels been me and Jess. I don't much care about records... all I want to do is help us beat Forest, and if I score, that would be a bonus."

WBA: Godden; Mulligan, Statham, T. Brown, Wile, Robertson, Martin, A. Brown (Cunningham), Regis, Trewick, Johnston.

Nottingham Forest: Shilton; Bowyer, Clark, McGovern, Needham, Burns, O'Neill, Gemmill, Withe, Woodcock, Robertson.

Attendance: 36,506

Before kick-off, against a team managed by one of football's most charismatic characters, Brian Clough, Albion's Ron Atkinson told his players: "You mustn't stand off and respect them; get in and get at them." And they did just that!

But Forest looked the more composed side during the early exchanges and Martin O'Neill forced two fine saves from Godden in the space of three minutes, but against the run of play, Albion took the lead in the 15th minute. Frank Clark brought Johnston down when the winger was in full flight and, from Derek Statham's long free-kick, Tony Brown helped the ball on to Martin who lobbed Peter Shilton with a well-timed and superbly executed volley.

A slip by Kenny Burns soon afterwards let in Ally Brown but his effort went wide – he should have done better. Brown then saw another shot diverted clear by Shilton's foot.

The statistics stated that Forest had more possession in the first-half, but it was Albion who dictated the early stages of the second period, and in the 48th minute the crowd saw a goal of pure brilliance.

Mulligan delivered a long ball out of defence. It bounced away from Dave Needham and, with the Forest back-line rather spread-eagled, Cyrille raced into space to rifle a shot beyond the diving Shilton. This was a remarkable strike from a player who a year earlier was playing non-League football for Hayes and working as an electrician.

Albion, two goals to the good, didn't rest on their laurels, and Forest were pushed back, as first Cyrille and then Tony Brown tested Shilton. Clough started to panic and he sent six players forward, it was seven in one attack. Godden saved brilliantly from Peter Withe and Needham while Mulligan cleared another effort off the line.

For all their efforts, treble chasing Forest simply couldn't break through… Albion held on to register a famous victory. Manager Atkinson said: "We were brilliant, fantastic… and a bit more."

Cyrille recalled: "That was some win… and we thoroughly deserved it."

In the semi-final, Albion were paired with Ipswich Town, managed by former Hawthorns' favourite Bobby Robson. The venue was Highbury – unfortunately not a happy hunting ground for the Baggies. After losing there to Preston North End in the 1937 FA Cup semi-final, they had only managed four times in the last 40 years on Arsenal's ground.

Forest went on to win the Championship and lift the League Cup. In fact, they didn't lose another game all season, and actually went 57 more matches before suffering their next defeat – in a League game at Anfield on 9 December 1978.

6: FA Cup Semi-final

IPSWICH TOWN 3 WEST BROMWICH ALBION 1

8 April 1978

Cyrille believed – so do thousands of Albion supporters – that manager Ron Atkinson made a huge mistake by leaving Laurie Cunningham and Bryan Robson out of the team for the FA Cup semi-final encounter with Ipswich Town at Highbury. Laurie was on the bench, but not Robbo.

A week before the game Albion had won 1-0 at Leicester, although a fortnight earlier they had crashed 4-0 to Arsenal on the same Highbury pitch! That defeat by the Gunners was, in fact, only their second in their last 10 League games, and overall their performances had been good, although Cyrille had been finding it tough to find the net.

He had managed just five League goals all season, only one in his last 18 appearances, but with Tony Brown doing the business up front, Albion were confident of reaching their first FA Cup final for a decade.

Ipswich, managed by former Albion star Bobby Robson, were 11th in Division One at the time (Albion were 8th) and had lost four of their previous 10 League games and, in fact, had won just one since the turn of the year.

On route to the semi-final of the Cup, the Tractormen had avoided all the big guns, defeating Cardiff City 2-0, Hartlepool United 4-1,

Bristol Rovers 3-0 (after a 2-2 draw) and Millwall 6-1. And in their line-up they had future Albion player-manager Brian Talbot.

Both teams were given – and sold – 16,000 tickets and for Albion it was their record 18th appearance in a semi-final of this competition. For Ipswich it was their second, having lost their first to West Ham United in 1975.

Ipswich Town: Cooper; Burley, Mills, Talbot (Lambert), Hunter, Beattie, Osborne, Wark, Mariner, Turner, Woods.

WBA: Godden; Mulligan, Statham, T. Brown, Wile (Cunningham), Robertson, Martin, A. Brown, Regis, Trewick, Johnston.

Attendance: 50,922

A few days before the final, Albion manager Ron Atkinson had gone to Wembley with the BBC to film a piece for *Football Focus* (to be shown on the day of the final). And as the players sat and watched the TV, they were aghast when they saw him holding up the Cup. Skipper John Wile said, in no uncertain terms: "He's set us up good and proper here." Meanwhile, Ipswich boss Robson said to his players as they watched the programme: "Look at him… he thinks he's won it already." That fired his team up with doubt!

Both teams started nervously with passes going astray but Albion looked the more inventive, with Willie Johnston probing down the left.

But then, against the run of play, Ipswich scored on eight minutes. Breaking quickly down Albion's right, the experienced Paddy Mulligan was caught out big time as Mick Mills went on the overlap and from the full-back's cross, Talbot threw himself in front of John Wile to head the ball goalwards. Tony Godden got a hand to it but couldn't prevent it from entering the net via the crossbar.

Both Wile and Talbot had to leave the field for treatment for serious head injuries. Wile returned to the field but Talbot didn't, eventually being replaced by Mick Lambert.

Albion went in search of an equaliser and, after Cyrille had headed wide, Ipswich scored again in the 19th minute. Lambert swung over a corner from the right, the ball was flicked on by Paul Mariner and when Cyrille failed to cut it out, Mills swooped to hook it past a stranded Godden.

This was a stunner… but with Atkinson urging his troops on from the touchline, Albion went on the offensive and before half-time Cyrille had a powerful header saved by Paul Cooper under the bar.

With Wile struggling with his vision (his head swathed in bandages and blood streaming down his face) Albion continued to push forward after the break but on the hour mark, against his wishes, skipper Wile was withdrawn and Cunningham sent on.

Gradually Albion worked up crisper momentum, but then it was learned that Johnston had been carrying a shoulder injury from very early on and was in some pain. The Scot, though, battled on and with 15 minutes remaining, following a free-kick awarded for a professional foul on Cunningham, centre-half Allan Hunter, under pressure from Cyrille, handled inside the penalty area. Welsh referee Clive Thomas immediately pointed to the spot, allowing Tony Brown to smash home the 12-yard kick. Albion were back in business and, soon afterwards, Johnston missed with a clear header, putting the ball wide… if it had fallen to Cyrille, it would have been 2-2.

Albion were now in control of the game and knowing that they had come back from two down in a League match at Ipswich just five weeks earlier, believed they could do the same again at Highbury.

But then, on 85 minutes, Mick Martin received a second yellow card and was sent off – the first dismissal in an FA Cup semi-final for 48 years – since Arthur Childs took an early bath playing for Hull City against Arsenal in 1930. This left Albion a mountain to climb and, right at the death, John Wark rubbed salt into the Baggies' wounds by powering home Clive Woods' corner to seal a 3-1 win for Ipswich.

The Albion players left the field heads bowed and totally distraught. Tony Brown said: "It hurts so much to be a loser at this stage of the competition."

Johnston recalled: "It was desolation in our dressing at the end of the game. And I just don't know how I managed to head wide with the score at 2-1."

Cyrille added: "We didn't give a good account of ourselves. It would have been easier to take the defeat if we had played well, but we didn't; we were terrible really."

Returning to the Midlands on the team bus, Cyrille recalled the journey: "We were all quiet – it was a like a morgue. Watching our fans in cars and on coaches travelling along the motorway with us, staring into space… it was so painful."

Ipswich went on to beat Arsenal 1-0 in the final at Wembley, Roger Osborne the goalscorer.

7: Football League Division One

MANCHESTER CITY 1 WEST BROMWICH ALBION 3

15 April 1978

Albion had bounced back after their FA Cup elimination at the hands of Ipswich by beating Newcastle United 2-0 at The Hawthorns with goals from Cyrille and a rare one from Paddy Mulligan, his first for the Baggies.

Next up for Ron Atkinson's men was a seemingly tough encounter at Maine Road against Tony Book's Manchester City who, at the time, were sitting third in the table. Albion hadn't won on City soil for 10 years and, in the home side's ranks, and playing well, was former 'Baggie' Asa Hartford along with two future Albion stars, midfielder Gary Owen and winger Peter Barnes.

John Wile was still side-lined with his head injury, so Bryan Robson continued at the heart of the defence, alongside Ally Robertson. And with both teams chasing a UEFA Cup place there was a lot at stake.

Manchester City: Corrigan; Clements, Booth (Palmer), Watson, Doyle, Power, Channon, Hartford, Owen, Kidd, Barnes.

WBA: Godden; Mulligan, Statham, T. Brown, Robson, Robertson, Cantello, A. Brown, Regis, Trewick, Cunningham.

Attendance: 36,521

City came close to taking the lead on nine minutes. Barnes beat Mulligan and crossed into the danger-zone where Brian Kidd, diving forward, saw his header rebound off an upright with 'keeper Godden beaten. The ball came out to Mick Channon but his effort sailed way over the bar.

Albion were pinned in their own half for quite a while but on 22 minutes Cyrille scored a brilliant goal to give the Baggies the lead.

Intercepting a crossfield pass by Owen to Barnes some 20 yards inside his own half of the field, Cyrille set off a mesmerising run which took him past Kidd, then Mick Doyle and Tommy Booth and, after holding off a sturdy challenge by Paul Power, he moved on to steer the ball past Joe Corrigan and into the corner of the net.

"Certainly the greatest goal I've ever seen," said former City manager Joe Mercer. "This boy could be the next Dixie Dean"… high praise indeed from a player who starred behind Dean during his days as an Everton player in the 1930s.

Even Cyrille couldn't believe what he had done! And after the match he said: "Their defence just opened up and went all the way. It was as simple as that."

In later years, he admitted that this effort against City was one of the best goals he ever scored.

Five minutes after going one up, Albion stunned the home crowd by taking a two-goal lead.

Cyrille found Len Cantello out on the City right with a measured pass. The midfielder's cross was headed goalwards by Tony Brown but Corrigan produced a fine save, pushing the ball onto a post. However, quickest to react was Laurie Cunningham, who gleefully volleyed home in superb fashion.

Three magnificent saves by Corrigan from John Trewick before half-time and Tony Brown and Ally Brown early in the second-half, prevented Albion from running away with the game.

But having said that, City fell three behind in the 68th minute when Ally Brown, taking Trewick's pass in his stride, rounded big Dave Watson before banging the ball past the diving City 'keeper.

Why oh why couldn't Albion have played like this in their previous away game against Ipswich?

Further chances fell to Cyrille and Tony Brown as City looked demoralised and, with the home fans groaning, Cunningham saw an effort fizz inches wide. But, surprisingly, City somehow perked up.

Barnes cracked a drive against the angle of crossbar and post (when he should have scored) and Godden saved brilliantly from Kidd. Then, with just five minutes remaining, and the ground emptying fast, Kidd pulled a goal back for the hosts. Up with his attackers, defender Watson scooped the ball into the air for Kidd to head home via an upright.

Manager Atkinson's comments after this excellent display were refreshing: "We had pace, determination, composure and the will to win." And Ally Brown butted in by saying: "Cyrille and Laurie were outstanding. I thought I was pretty quick, but they were like greyhounds, Cyrille in particular."

Albion won their next game at home to Derby 1-0, courtesy of Tony Brown's 74th minute penalty, but succumbed 3-0 to rivals Aston Villa four days later, also at The Hawthorns. The recovered to beat Everton at home 3-1 with another stunning goal from Cyrille, drew 1-1 at Norwich and ended the season with a 2-2 home draw with the champions Nottingham Forest.

By finishing 6th in the First Division, and after Liverpool had beaten FC Brugge in the European Cup final, it was confirmed that Albion had qualified for next season's UEFA Cup competition, along with City who had taken fourth place in the table.

Next on the agenda for Cyrille and Albion were a couple of testimonial matches (for Swindon Town legend Don Rogers and ex-Baggies' goalkeeper John Osborne) followed by an historic tour of China.

8: China Tour Friendly

PEKING XI 1 WEST BROMWICH ALBION 3

17 May 1978

On 12 May 1978, a squad of 17 West Bromwich Albion players, nine club officials, a 'World in Action' TV film crew, along with top presenter Julian Pettifer, a dozen or so guests of the Society for Anglo-Chinese Understanding, plus a handful of journalists, flew out of Heathrow airport to Hong Kong via Rome, Bahrain and Calcutta, for a prestigious 'friendly and goodwill' tour of the Far East.

Four games (three booked in advance) were played in the People's Republic of China with one more contested on the return journey.

The three fixtures initially on the menu were, firstly, against a Peking XI in mid-May, a second versus the China national team 48 hours later and a third against a Shanghai XI on 22 May. Albion then participated in a fourth match (not pre-arranged) against a side representing Kwantung Province in Canton on 26 May, before the fifth and final encounter, in Hong Kong, two days later.

No other professional football team from anywhere in the world had previously won a game in China, but Albion quickly created history with a 3-1 victory in their opening fixture in a Peking XI in front of 80,000 fans. The Baggies followed up with 2-0 wins over the host country in front of an 89,400 crowd and against Shanghai when 40,000 spectators turned out, before hammering Kwantung

Province 6-0 with 30,500 present. Cyrille scored in each of those first four games, totalling five goals overall, and Wolverhampton-based World Cup referee Jack Taylor officiated in all four fixtures. Albion rounded off their tour with a 3-0 victory over a tough Hong Kong XI on 28 May, when, once again, Cyrille found the net.

Cyrille and Laurie Cunningham were the stars in the eyes of the Chinese supporters... they had never seen black footballers perform so magnificently as the Albion duo.

I have chosen Albion's first win in China as one of Cyrille's 'Fifty Defining Fixtures'... as it was a special occasion for him personally and also for the club.

Peking XI: Chi Sei-Un; Chen Wen-Heung, Wang Sin-Shen, Li Yei Shaw, Leun Chin-Lu (Li Hun-yi), Wen Yuan, Shah Pau-Chu, Cha Oui-Hua (Ches Si-ten), Chi E-Wang, Li Teh-Li (Ling Li-Fu), Hung Wang-San.

WBA: Godden (Grew); Batson, Statham, T. Brown, Wile, Robertson, Martin, Robson, Regis (W. Hughes), A. Brown (Summerfield), Cunningham (Monaghan).

Attendance; 80,000

There was a huge crowd inside the Workers Stadium in Peking to see Albion's opening game. Despite 48 hours of rain (sometimes heavy) the pitch was in very good condition, although somewhat uneven in places.

John Trewick led Albion onto the field, with a Union Jack flag being carried in front of him. And it was 'Tucka' who had the first shot of the game, driving wide from 20 yards.

Albion controlled the first-half quite comfortably although they didn't create too many chances, Cyrille and Cunningham going closest.

The breakthrough arrived a minute before the interval. Tony Brown conjured up some space on the right and from his accurate cross, Cyrille, brushing in front of his marker, netted with a strong, well-directed header from 10 yards.

Sixty seconds into the second-half it was 2-0 when Ally Brown, in space, beat goalkeeper Chi Sei-Un after some neat interplay involving Mick Martin, Bryan Robson and Cyrille.

But the hosts responded and in the 53rd minute, Li Teh-Li charged down Ally Robertson's attempted clearance, ran forward, unchallenged, and as Godden left his line, he coolly slipped the ball past him and into an empty goal. Loud applause only greeted the goal.

Albion came again and after two near misses, one from Cyrille, the other by Martin, they made the game safe with 20 minutes remaining.

Derek Statham – still recovering from a high tackle by Li Yei Shaw that had knocked him almost semi-conscious – slipped in Cunningham who, looking up, crossed perfectly for Ally Brown to hammer a fierce right-footed shot into the net from near the penalty spot

In fact, a groggy-looking Statham was left with stud marks on his chest and forehead – and English referee Jack Taylor thought the challenge was accidental!

Soon afterwards, Cunningham was substituted by Kevin Summerfield and, with his first touch of the ball, he almost scored, home 'keeper Chi Sei-Un saving at the foot of his right-hand post. Another Baggies' sub, Derek Monghan, also came close to finding the net late on, while at the other end of the field, Mark Grew, who had replaced Godden, saved well from Hung Wang-San.

"The Chinese played better than I expected," said Albion manager Ron Atkinson, reflecting on what, at the time, was an historical victory – as Albion became the first 'senior professional' football team to win in the People's Republic of China.

And, of course, it was during the early part of this tour that Albion midfielder John Trewick admitted: "Once you've seen one wall, you've seen them all"... as the party walked around, and on, the famous Great Wall of China.

Summing up the tour, Tony Brown said: "China was so bad – I've never seen poverty like it. We wanted to go home after the first day."

Cyrille was not impressed either, saying: "It wasn't a great place at all. Strangely, for Laurie, Brendon and me, most Chinese had never seen black people before, so when we walked past, they tried to touch our hair."

And Bryan Robson, when interviewed, said: "I would rather have gone to Alicante!"

Skipper John Wile recalled: "We were determined not to be beaten. We were representing club and country, so we took matches seriously, although the atmosphere was surreal – very quiet despite huge crowds. Before our first match we were taken to a domestic game and, at one stage, there was a murmur from the crowd, like you might get from the Brummie Road End, and immediately an announcement was made asking the crowd to be quiet because they would put the players off!"

And Derek Statham told me: "It was great at the time, although a bit boring. I don't think I will go back."

On 1 August 1979, a team from China visited The Hawthorns for a 'return fixture'. A crowd of 11,382 saw Albion win 4-0 with Lin Lua-fang (own-goal), Cyrille, Ally Brown and Peter Barnes the scorers in a rather one-sided match.

9: UEFA Cup 1st Round 1st Leg

GALATASARAY SPOR KÜLÜBU 1
WEST BROMWICH ALBION 3

13 September 1978

Unbeaten in their opening five League games of the season, as well as keeping two clean-sheets in draws with Leeds United in the League Cup, Albion were in good form ahead of their first competitive European game outside the UK for almost 10 years – since visiting Romania to play Dinamo Bucharest in the Cup-winners' Cup in November 1968.

For each and every selected team member – except for Tony Brown who had played in European competitions for the Baggies in 1966 and 1968 – this was their first trip abroad for a major football match and, as manager, Ron Atkinson said: "They're all up for it."

Initially, the match against Galatasaray in Turkey was scheduled to be played in Istanbul but due to crowd trouble during a UEFA Cup encounter the previous season, it was switched 250 miles south of the country to the Ataturk Stadium in Izmir. The Albion party stayed in an 'awful' hotel and Atkinson, in fact, gave his team talk in a street corner café drinking a cup of coffee!

As for Cyrille... he had netted only one of the nine goals Albion had scored in their early season matches but admitted: "I'm fit and I know the goals will arrive sooner rather than later."

Galatasaray SK: Eser; Erdogan, Müfit, Mehmet Tanman, Güngör, Turgay (Ergucu), Fatih, Ömer, Ali Yavuz, Mehmet Oguz, Gökmen.

WBA: Godden; Batson, Statham, Cunningham, Wile, Robertson, Cantello, A. Brown, Regis, Trewick, Robson.

Attendance: 38,443

With Willie Johnston suspended from all UEFA competitions, manager Atkinson elected to pack his midfield by bringing in John Trewick. And after the hassle of getting to the ground, arriving there with only minutes to spare, due to traffic congestion around the city's one-way system, Albion went out and registered an excellent victory.

In fact, the Baggies started off like a house on fire and after Cyrille had gone close early on, Bryan Robson found space inside the penalty area to fire his side into the lead after just eight minutes.

With Laurie Cunningham causing all sorts of problems with his speed and clever footwork, the home defenders were all over the place and when Ally Brown tried a shot, the ball somehow flew wide of Eser Ozaltindere's right hand post off the heel of Güngör Tekin. Soon afterwards, another effort from Cyrille was a fraction too high.

Galatasaray managed only two worthwhile attacks in the first-half which was dominated entirely by Albion who should have scored at least twice more but for good saves from Eser, while Len Cantello and Cunningham both missed the target from good positions.

After taking stock of the situation early in the second-half, Albion moved up a gear and scored a fine second goal in the 62nd minute through Cunningham.

Brendon Batson made ground down the right wing and when his low cross came flying into the danger-zone, Cyrille completely wrong-footed the home defence by stepping over the ball, allowing Cunningham to drive it into the net from 10 yards.

Five minutes later 'Man of the Match' Cunningham made it three-nil. Collecting a clever pass from Cantello, he charged at the Galatasaray back line, leaving two players for dead before striking the ball right-footed around the 'keeper and high into the net with great precision and accuracy.

"It was a magical goal," said Cyrille.

Galatasaray, to their credit, didn't lie down and with barely two minutes remaining, Romanian referee Francisco Kolossi awarded them a penalty when Tony Godden was adjudged to have brought down Fatih Terim. The Turkish player actually ran into TG! Fatih got up and dusted himself down before banging home the spot-kick… to the delight of the home supporters!

Albion became the first British team to beat Galatasaray in Turkey and their feat was not equalled until 1999-2000 when Chelsea triumphed in a Champions League game.

Albion, fielding an unchanged team, comfortably won the return leg at The Hawthorns with an identical score-line, to go through to the second round 6-2 on aggregate. Cunningham (penalty) and Robson were again on target, along with 'Tucka' Trewick.

Next up for Cyrille and Co. was a League encounter away at Chelsea, while in the next round of the UEFA Cup, Albion were drawn against the Portuguese club, Sporting Braga.

10: Football League Division One

LEEDS UNITED 1 WEST BROMWICH ALBION 3

14 October 1978

Twelve days after losing to Leeds United in a League Cup second round, second replay, and also suffering a 1-0 home defeat at the hands of Tottenham Hotspur, Albion travelled to Elland Road to take on the Yorkshire club in a First Division match, for what would be their fourth meeting in the space of just five weeks.

Leeds had just lost their manager, Jock Stein, who had been tempted away to take over as head coach of Scotland and were all set to appoint ex-Burnley wing-half Jimmy Anderson as their new boss. League champions four years earlier, they were not playing at all well and, in fact, were languishing in 13th place in the table with Albion up as high as sixth.

Tony Currie, who had missed five League games in a row, returned to the Leeds midfield, while Albion had Len Cantello back to partner Bryan Robson in the engine room.

Ron Atkinson's team had already scored 15 goals in their nine League games with Cyrille and Laurie Cunningham bagging four apiece.

Leeds United: Harvey; Stevenson, Cherry, Flynn, Hart, Madeley, E. Gray, Hankin, F. Gray, Currie, Graham.

WBA: Godden; Batson, Statham (Johnston), Cunningham, Wile, Robertson, Robson, A. Brown, Regis, Cantello, T. Brown.

Attendance: 25,931

Leeds started well but immediately one could see that Currie was not 100 per cent fit and after a challenge by Cantello he had to receive some on-field treatment by the trainer.

Albion had the first effort on goal – a long range shot by Ally Brown which was easily gathered by David Harvey. Leeds responded with a snap shot from Ray Hankin while Baggies' 'keeper Tony Godden comfortably dealt with a header from Arthur Graham.

On 20 minutes the home side took the lead. Trevor Cherry's long high free-kick was not cleared and, after a bit of a scramble deep inside the Albion penalty area and Graham had swung his right boot at the ball, it fell to Byron Stevenson who sent it fizzing past Godden and into the net from six yards.

Although stunned to a certain degree, Albion went on the offensive and after Cyrille (twice) and Cunningham had both gone close to equalising, they eventually drew level five minutes before half-time. Brendon Batson slipped a clever pass to Cantello, who quickly moved the ball into the path of Tony Brown. The Albion hit man strode forward and from fully 25 yards struck a blistering shot into Harvey's net via an upright. This was Bomber's 209th League goal for Albion – making him the club's leading scorer of all-time, ahead of Ronne Allen. He was congratulated by each and every one of his team-mates, even Godden, on a wonderful achievement.

It was now game on, and with Albion in total control, and Cantello bossing midfield, Leeds were pegged back in their own half, as Cyrille and Ally Brown almost breached their defence for a second time.

Albion continued to dictate the play early in the second-half although Godden had to be on his toes to save from Cherry and Graham, while Robertson headed a dangerous cross from Eddie Gray over his own crossbar.

Albion, despite having the lion's share of possession simply couldn't grab a second goal, and with the referee Kevin McNally's watch slowly ticking down, a draw seemed the likely outcome.

But then a piece of magic from Cyrille lit up the afternoon for the Baggies and their travelling fans. On 83 minutes, he showed great pace and wonderful control as he latched onto Cunningham's exquisite pass from the right before firing home hard and low past Harvey. And then, with barely 90 seconds remaining, the big fella scored again.

Winger Willie Johnston, who had come on as a substitute for Derek Statham, weaved inside full-back Stevenson before squaring the ball across the penalty area for Cyrille who fired home in style to sew up an excellent 3-1 victory. Right at the death Johnston almost sneaked in a fourth.

This victory set Albion up nicely for their trip to Portugal to take on Sporting Braga in the first leg of a second round UEFA Cup tie. And back to form Albion won again, this time by 2-0 with Cyrille netting both goals. 'Smokin' Joe' was on fire… next up Coventry City at The Hawthorns.

11: Football League Division One

WEST BROMWICH ALBION 7 COVENTRY CITY 1

21 October 1978

Fresh from a 2-0 UEFA Cup win in Portugal, it was back to League action for Albion in the form of a Midlands derby against one of Cyrille's future clubs, Coventry City, managed by the former Liverpool wing-half Gordon Milne. And at the heart of the Sky Blues' defence was Scotsman Jim Holton, who seven years earlier had been released by the then Baggies' manager Alan Ashman on a free transfer to Shrewsbury Town.

Also lining up for City was Ernie Hunt, who became famous for his 'donkey kick' goal against Everton.

Albion, with a home League win for two months (since beating Bolton Wanderers 4-0 at the end of August) were unchanged for the third game in a row.

Three of the last four League games between Albion and City had ended in draws including a 3-3 encounter at The Hawthorns just six months earlier.

At the time of kick-off, Albion were lying fourth in the table with Coventry (beaten only once by Liverpool) three places below them in seventh.

WBA: Godden; Batson, Statham, Cunningham, Wile, Robertson, Robson, A. Brown, Regis, Cantello (Johnston), T. Brown.

Coventry City: Sealey; Coop, McDonald, Yorath, Holton (Green), Gillespie, Hutchison, Wallace, Ferguson, Powell, Hunt.

Attendance: 27,381

After taking the field in a shocking strip of all chocolate, can you picture the headlines: City melt away, City meltdown, Sky Blues licked, as Milne's men were slaughtered to the tune of 7-1 and, in reality, the final score-line could, and should, have been in double figures, so well did Albion play, or should that be so poorly did Coventry perform?

After a rather slowish start – two shots by Albion, none by City – the floodgates opened in the 14th minute when Tony Brown fed in Len Cantello on the right side of the penalty area. The angle for a shot at goal looked too tight, but the midfielder let fly with a strong low drive, and was delighted to see the ball bounce awkwardly in front of Les Sealey and high into the net. This was Cantello's first League goal for two years, since his strike in a 4-0 home win over Manchester United in October 1976.

In the 29th minute, after a period of Albion pressure, City fell two behind. A speculative downfield clearance by Brendon Batson caught Mick Coop off guard. The ball was collected by Cunningham who set off at pace before cutting in from the left to steer the ball over the advancing Sealey.

Three-and-a-half minutes later, it was three nil to the Baggies. Cantello sent Tony Brown clear down the right and from his excellent cross, Cyrille, moving in for the kill, was first to the ball, heading it powerfully into the net from eight yards.

Albion were applauded off the field at half-time, well in control and with their tails up.

And it got worse for the visitors just past the hour mark. After Ally Brown had gone close and Harrow referee Clive White had turned down a penalty appeal, Tony Brown's corner was flicked on by John Wile to Cunningham who, arriving late at the far post, thumped his header past Sealey.

The City goalkeeper then pulled off a stunning save when Cyrille released a thunderbolt.

With Albion pressing forward at will, this one-sided game suddenly changed course in the 70th minute when City broke away for Mick Ferguson to side-foot home substitute Alan Green's cross past Godden from close range to make it 4-1.

This was only a hiccup as far as Albion was concerned and, six minutes later, Bryan Robson tapped a short free-kick into Tony Brown's path. Say no more… the 'Bomber' let fly, sending the ball screaming into the top corner of Sealey's net from 20 yards.

Albion's sixth goal, in the 82nd minute, was scored, and deservedly so, by Cyrille. He picked up the ball near the halfway line, shot past a bemused Barry Powell, went round Gary Gillespie and Coop, before thumping the ball home from 18 yards. With time running out, Derek Statham ventured upfield and after Terry Yorath had lost possession, he went on to wallop in Albion's seventh and final goal with a vicious left-footer.

Statham's goal, in fact, had a touch of irony about it. Normally, he would have backed himself with a fiver against Atkinson's odds of 14-1 against him scoring.

"I did it to encourage Derek to go forward," said 'Big Ron' who added: "This week he didn't take the bet and it saved me 70 quid." It could easily have been 'seventh heaven' for Statham!

Cyrille's comments after this big win summed up Albion's performance: "We hammered 'em good and proper. We could have doubled our score quite easily."

In The Hawthorns' press room after the match, Coventry boss Milne admitted: "This is the first time as manager I have felt humiliated. My players were an utter disgrace."

Albion chief Atkinson had told his players to be ruthless. "This was murder," he said.

Later in the season, Albion knocked Coventry out of the FA Cup, winning 4-0 at The Hawthorns after a 2-2 draw at Highfield Road, and they also completed their first ever League double over the Sky Blues with a 3-1 away victory

This was Albion's biggest League win for almost 11 years; in November 1967 they whipped Burnley 8-1 at The Hawthorns.

12: 'B' International Friendly

CZECHOSLOVAKIA 'B' 0 ENGLAND 'B' 1

28 November 1978

England did not play a 'B' international between February 1957 and February 1978 but once Ron Greenwood had taken over as manager (from Don Revie), he quickly arranged such a game against a strong West German side in Augsburg, which England lost 2-1. Next up was a 1-1 draw with Malaysia 'B' in a friendly in Kuala Lumpur in May 1978, followed by three 'B' internationals on tour to New Zealand in June 1978, all of which were won.

Before Greenwood reintroduced 'B' games, England's last such fixture resulted in a 4-1 win over Scotland in front of almost 40,000 fans at St Andrew's, Birmingham, in early February 1957. Albion's right-back Don Howe lined up for England, along with the likes of Brian Clough, Peter Sillett (whose brother John would be coaching Cyrille at Coventry City in 40 years' time), Tony Marchi, Trevor Smith, Harry Hooper and Brian Pilkington.

Prior to this friendly game in Prague, England had played 24 previous 'B' internationals. They had won 13, drawn five and lost six. Their best win was 5-0 over Switzerland in Sheffield in 1950 while their heaviest had been 7-1 in France in 1952. They also lost 5-0 to Italy in 1950.

Twenty-four hours before this game, the full England team took on, and beat, the Czechs 1-0 in a senior international at Wembley. Could the 'reserves' follow suit?

Czechoslovakia: Koubek; Dvorak (P. Nemec), R. Nemec, Vaclavicek, Macela, Briza (Kloucek), Rott, Licka, Mazura (Kunzo), Caloun, Novak.

England: Corrigan (Manchester City); Gidman (Aston Villa), Sansom (Crystal Palace), B. Greenhoff (Manchester United) – sub. Hazell (Wolverhampton Wanderers); Lyons (Everton), Talbot (Ipswich Town), Cunningham (West Bromwich Albion), Sunderland (Arsenal), Mortimer (Aston Villa) – sub. Owen (Manchester City); Flanagan (Charlton Athletic) – sub. Regis (West Bromwich Albion); Daley (Wolverhampton Wanderers).

Attendance: 4,996

This game in Prague was not a great football match but for Cyrille it was another step up the ladder towards the full England team. Although he was named as a substitute, he was told, "Don't worry you'll get on before the end."

He had, of course, played in an U21 international just nine weeks earlier against Denmark but this time round he knew that a good performance (when he did get on) would do him no harm whatsoever when the selectors met to name their squad for the European Championship qualifier against Northern Ireland at Wembley in February.

As it was neither side played well in a rather lackadaiscal first-half. Mick Flanagan and Steve Daley had England's two best efforts – both off target – while goalkeeper Joe Corrigan saved well from one of Czechoslovakia's brightest players, Oldrich Rott.

Both teams used their full quota of three substitutes for the second-half… and as soon as Cyrille came onto the field, he saw a vicious shot saved low down by Josef Koubek.

The vital breakthrough was made in the 56th minute. Attacking through the middle, England had six players inside the Czech half of the field when the ball broke to Daley, who struck a sweet right-footed shot low into the net from just outside the penalty area.

After the Wolves player had seen another effort fizz narrowly wide of the target a minute later, Cyrille just couldn't stretch his right leg out far enough when Alan Sunderland's cross flew across the penalty area from the right.

The home side threw everything bar the kitchen sink at the England defence during the last quarter-of-an-hour, but they couldn't conjure up an equaliser, partly due to some solid tackling by Bob Hazell and one timely clearance from inside his own six-yard area by Brian Talbot.

England held on, just… and as for Cyrille, he thought he did well considering the time he had on the pitch! But unfortunately he was not called up by manager Ron Greenwood for the Irish game, Bob Latchford of Everton being preferred alongside Kevin Keegan up front. Cyrille would have to wait until February 1982 before making his senior international debut – against Northern Ireland at Wembley!

The England quartet against the Czechs of Corrigan, Mortimer, Talbot and Owen would all be associated with Cyrille's first club, West Bromwich Albion in later years.

13: UEFA Cup, 3rd Round, 2nd Leg

WEST BROMWICH ALBION 2 VALENCIA 0
(Albion won 3-1 on aggregate)

6 December 1978

Three weeks before taking on La Liga club Valencia in the second leg of their third round UEFA Cup tie, Albion had gone to Spain and played brilliantly in front of almost 48,000 spectators inside the Mestilla Stadium to earn a creditable 1-1 draw, courtesy of a superb equaliser from Laurie Cunningham.

Albion had fallen behind in the 14th minute when Tony Godden failed to collect a corner and allowed the Argentinean Daniel Felman to head home from close range.

But Albion were never second best and matched their rivals kick for kick, pass for pass, tackle for tackle, and deservedly earned a draw with Cunningham's goal three minutes into the second-half.

Baggies' boss Ron Atkinson said after the game: "We should have paralysed them. When did you last hear an English team being cheered off a foreign football pitch? Cunningham's performance reminded me of George Best."

Team-mate Ally Brown was amazed by Cunningham's display, saying, "He played a game that I've never seen anybody play in my life."

And there is no doubt that his performance against Valencia got him his big money move to Real Madrid.

Before the second leg Albion had been held 1-1 at home by Aston Villa in a League game, but they were quietly confident of seeing off their Spanish opponents under The Hawthorns floodlights.

WBA: Godden; Batson, Statham, T. Brown, Wile, Robertson, Robson, A. Brown, Regis, Cantello (Trewick), Cunningham.

Valencia: Manzanedo; Carrete, Cordero, Arias, Botubot, Bonhof, Suara, Cabral (Diarte), Felman, Solsona, Kempes.

Attendance: 35,034

After enjoying the Spanish sunshine and playing on a lush green pitch in Valencia, the conditions were completely different at The Hawthorns… it was bitterly cold and the slightly uneven pitch was frozen hard. In fact, French referee Robert Wurz only decided to give the game the go-ahead an hour or so before kick-off. One quickly knew that the Spanish team wasn't too familiar with these sorts of conditions!

Valencia (Els Taranges – The Oranges) came out with a plan… defend deep, tackle hard and often, give Albion no space in which to play and get tight on Cunningham. And these tactics were apparent from the word go when Juan Cordero cynically took Cyrille's legs from under him in the very first minute. No booking for the Spaniard though, just a ticking off!

Albion had started strongly and in the fourth minute they scored.

Derek Statham swung over a free-kick from the left and when the ball bounced awkwardly, it was handled by hard man Cordero. Tony Brown dutifully found the net from the spot, sending José Luis Manzanedo the wrong way. This was 'Bomber's' 60th penalty for Albion and his 50th first-time conversion, having seen two saved earlier in his career before netting the rebound.

The penalty decision clearly upset the Spaniards and, almost immediately, Cyrille was clobbered twice more in quick succession by Ricardo Arias who was yellow-carded for his second dreadful foul.

Early substitutes Carlos Diarte and José Carrete were also booked for committing outrageous fouls on Cunningham and Bryan Robson respectively.

Albion, although in charge, were not being given too much space in the middle of the pitch but with Messrs Wile and Robertson looking strong at the back and containing the threat of Bonhof and Kempes, the Baggies still created chances, Cyrille and then Ally Brown both going close before half-time while 'Bomber' Brown had a goal disallowed when he touched Cyrille's glancing ahead past Manzanedo from an offside position.

The same player was then flagged offside again when Statham netted in the 48th minute but after Bonhof had seen a 25-yarder zip past Godden's post early in the second period, Albion never looked back. Robson, Cantello (and then substitute John Trewick) took charge of midfield and, with Cunningham posing a huge threat down both flanks, Valencia were always on the back foot.

Then, in the 79th minute, it was game over when Albion scored a second goal.

Wile intercepted a long pass from Manuel Angel Botubot deep inside his own half. The Baggies' skipper quickly delivered a long ball upfield towards Cyrille who chested it down and, as Carrete dived in (again), the ball broke loose to Cunningham. He shot off down the right, skipped past another crude challenge from back-tracking Carrete, reached the bye-line and crossed perfectly for Tony Brown who, with unerring accuracy volleyed home past the diving Manzanedo from near the penalty spot. His marker Botubot was caught in no man's land.

Graham Taylor, then manager of Watford, said after the game: "Brown made it look so easy – the timing of his shot was perfection. As for Cunningham, once again he showed class and confidence, but Brown was my 'Man of the Match' although big Cyrille pushed him hard. He must have more bruises on his body that a boxer after a 15 round battering."

Albion boss Ron Atkinson reckoned his players were 'far too tense' at times but still said it was "a handsome performance."

Cyrille recalled: "The atmosphere inside the ground before kick-off was terrific. We knew they (Valencia) didn't fancy playing on a hard pitch. We were up for it and we hammered 'em."

The away draw and home win over Valencia made it six UEFA Cup games without defeat for the Baggies – following two victories over Galatasaray and two more over Sporting Braga.

Next on their programme, a tough quarter-final, two legged encounter against Red Star Belgrade.

14: Football League Division One

MANCHESTER UNITED 3 WEST BROMWICH ALBION 5

30 December 1978

Albion, on a ten-match unbeaten run in the League, were in brilliant form when they travelled north to take on Manchester United at Old Trafford. Four days earlier they had won 2-1 at Arsenal, having beaten arch-rivals Wolves 3-0 at Molineux before that.

Manager Ron Atkinson was able to field an unchanged team for the fifth successive game, naming Willie Johnston, still not 100 per cent fit and after his traumas in the World Cup in Argentina, on the bench.

He knew his strikers were bang on form with the two Browns having already bagged 14 goals between them in the League, while Cyrille had netted nine and Cunningham six. He was certainly confident of winning despite being told that Albion had not beaten United at Old Trafford since 1959.

United were not playing well. They had been awful over Christmas, losing 3-0 at Bolton and by the same score at home to Liverpool. Earlier they had crashed 5-1 at Birmingham and had slipped down to eighth in the First Division table. Albion was third.

Manchester United: Bailey; B. Greenhoff, Houston, McIlroy, McQueen, Buchan, Coppell, J. Greenhoff (Sloan), Ritchie, McCreery, Thomas.

WBA: Godden; Batson, Statham, T. Brown, Wile, Robertson, Robson, A. Brown, Regis, Cantello, Cunningham.

Attendance: 45,091

One could easily fill four pages of this book reporting on this epic encounter at Old Trafford which was (and still is) described by many as the 'Match of the Century'.

Three goals were scored in three minutes, five in 12 and six in 25 during an exciting and exhilarating first-half, with two more following in the last quarter of an hour.

Albion, in their first worthwhile attack on five minutes, almost scored but Brendon Batson, in space, headed wide. United responded and Tony Godden had to be on his toes to cut out Steve Coppell's left wing cross.

In the 19th minute United's Andy Ritchie had a shot blocked on the line by Batson and when John Wile and Sammy McIlroy got in a tangle, Welsh referee Gwyn Owen started the game with a drop-ball 12 yards from Albion's goal line. After another melee, Godden touched Brian Greenhoff's lob over the bar.

However, from McIlroy's corner, Ally Brown's attempted clearance fell at the feet of the same Greenhoff brother who thumped home a 20-yard volley in off the crossbar to give United the lead.

Albion hit back and stunned the home side with two goals in the 26th and 27th minutes. Firstly, Cunningham, out on the left, fed in Tony Brown who guided a low left-footed shot past Gary Bailey, and then 50 seconds later, after a quick throw-in, a smart build-up involving Cunningham and Cyrille, resulted in the latter back-heeling the ball into the path of Len Cantello who smashed home an unstoppable shot from the edge of the penalty area. This was a terrific goal.

But Albion's joy was short lived! Within a minute United were level at 2-2 when Gordon McQueen powered home a header from Stewart Houston's free-kick on the left flank.

It was now all United at this juncture and in the 32nd minute they went back into the lead through Irish international midfielder McIlroy. After Robson had lost possession, the dangerous McIlroy somehow managed to weave his way in the danger-zone before crashing a right-footer, low into the net past Godden.

Albion, though, quickly regained their composure and went in search of an equaliser, which came seconds before half-time, and soon after Robson had been denied by Bailey.

Tony Brown, as menacing as ever, was on hand to slide Cantello's back-header from Derek Statham's chip, under Bailey from six yards. United didn't have time to kick off before the half-time whistle was blown.

Albion were quickly onto the front foot at the start of the second-half and Bailey had to go down smartly to collect Cantello's low swinging cross from the right.

United then forced two corners in quick succession which Albion dealt with and, in a rare venture upfield, Ally Robertson saw his powerful header cleared off United's goal line by Brian Greenhoff.

United came again and Godden steered a pile-driver from Ritchie over the bar. Then, after a clever Cunningham run and dribble, the ball broke to Cyrille who fired in a screaming 'banana shot' from 25 yards which produced a magnificent diving save from Bailey.

It was anyone's game and, in the end, it was Albion who prevailed. In the 76th minute, a long clearance by Godden, after he had gathered Mickey Thomas's shot, was headed on by Cyrille to Cunningham who sprinted clear of Houston and cleverly avoided Martin Buchan's desperate lunge, before driving the ball low past

Bailey to complete a brilliant solo effort and make it 4-3 to the Baggies.

Ninety seconds later Ally Brown skied a sitter over the top from two yards from Batson's cross, before Cyrille sewed up victory with a stunning fifth goal for Albion with six minutes remaining.

Cunningham once again sprinted clear of Houston down the right flank. He played in Ally Brown on the edge of the penalty area, and when Cyrille arrived on the scene, the Scot slipped the ball inside two defenders and into the path of 'Smokin' Joe' who did the rest in style, leaving McQueen for dead before crashing a ferocious right-footed shot high into the net past a bewildered Bailey.

This was justice for Cyrille who minutes earlier, following John Wile's free-kick, had seen another block-busting effort saved by United's goalkeeper.

The words 'Oh, what a goal… what a magnificent goal' shouted out by TV commentator Gerald Sinstadt summed up Cyrille's rocket-like effort to a tee. It was quite superb… watch it on YouTube.

After the game, Baggies' manager Ron Atkinson said: "That was one hell of a football match. There was not one punter who went away dissatisfied. If I had to choose the best goal it would have to be Cantello's. This was one of the most entertaining games I've ever watched. Bailey was their best player. He made some super saves in the second-half. A proper score would have been 10 for us. This was a red hot performance in Arctic conditions. Even the United fans in the end gave us a standing ovation – brilliant."

Cyrille said: "It was a wonderfully exciting game of football and the best team won by a mile." A few years later, Ally Brown admitted that this was the 'best game he ever played in'.

In fact, Cyrille, after an excellent all-round display and a terrific second-half, was named 'Man of the Match' and he duly received a magnum of champagne which was opened on the coach on the way down the M6 back to the Midlands.

Amazing Ally Brown failed to score in this game (or the 7-1 win over Coventry) yet still finished the season as Albion's leading marksman with a total of 24 goals in League and Cup.

15: UEFA Cup, 5th Round 2nd Leg

WEST BROMWICH ALBION 1 RED STAR BELGRADE 1
(Albion lost 2-1 on aggregate)

21 March 1979

After two legged victories over Galatasaray (6-2), Sporting Braga (3-0) and Valencia (3-1) in earlier rounds, Albion were confident of making it through to the semi-finals of the UEFA Cup at the expense of the Yugoslavian side Red Star Belgrade, despite losing the first leg 1-0.

Albion had not been at their best in Belgrade and were beaten by Dusko Savic's 84th minute vicious dipping strike which flew into the top corner of Tony Godden's net direct from a 20-yard free-kick awarded against John Wile who clearly got the ball first!

Manager Ron Atkinson wasn't at all happy with the decision, neither were several Albion players, Cyrille included who said: "No way did Wiley commit a foul. He won the ball fairly."

Ally Brown, standing in the wall when the free-kick was taken, recalled: "The speed it was going, and the way it went over our heads, I knew it was going in."

A crowd of 95,300 attended the first leg which was marred by fighting between rivals supporters from the two Belgrade clubs, Red Star and Partizan. One person was killed.

WBA: Godden; Batson, Statham, T. Brown, Wile, Robertson, Robson, A. Brown, Regis, Cantello, Cunningham.

Red Star: Stojanovic; Jovanovic, Krmptovic, Muslin, Jurisic, Jelikic, Sestic, Blagojevic, Savic, Borovnica, Milosavijevic.

Attendance: 31,110

The visitors made their clinical tactics clear for all to see, straight from the start, and, in fact, they gave away no less than seven free-kicks in the first 10 minutes of the game, and a not offending player was yellow-carded by East German referee Klaus Scheurell, who should certainly have cautioned Nicola Jovanovic (who later joined Manchester United), Slavoljub Muslin and Ivan Jurisic for outrageous fouls on Cunningham and Tony Brown respectively.

Early on, Cyrille sent 'Bomber' Brown racing through on goal but the club's all-time record marksman scuffed his shot, allowing Aleksandar Stojanovic to make a comfortable save.

After the referee had warned two more Red Star players about time wasting (even before the half hour mark had been reached) Cyrille and Cunningham both had half-chances before Albion deservedly took the lead in the 42nd minute.

Cvijetin Blagojevic committed his fourth foul of the night by bringing down Bryan Robson, and from Brendon Batson's free-kick Ally Brown jumped highest to flick the ball on towards Cyrille who, in the company of three defenders, swivelled superbly before finding the net with an excellent right-footed shot... a glorious goal, and it was just the tonic Albion needed.

They finished the half well and were looking good at the start of the second period as referee Scheurell got busy, again, this time cautioning Blagovic (at long last), Muslin (for a blatant bodycheck on 'Bomber' Brown) and Dusan Savic (foul) all in quick succession, with Cyrille taking the brunt of some ferocious tackling. In fact, even Cyrille himself was yellow-carded for reacting when fouled (for the umpteenth time).

Albion kept on pressing and, although chances were few and far between, they never looked like conceding either, with goalkeeper Tony Godden a virtual spectator.

With the aggregate score level at 1-1 and with extra-time looming, Albion looked the stronger team as the watch ticked down, but a lack of experience and certainly composure cost them dearly with just two minutes remaining.

With several Albion players seemingly too far upfield, the lively Muslin burst forward from the centre circle and fed Milos Sestic. He avoided two challenges and reached the edge of the penalty area where Baggies' defender Ally Robertson had a chance to clear the ball. But the rugged Scot tried to nick the ball away from the Yugoslav instead of giving it an almighty thump (perhaps into row Z) allowing Sestic to take aim and fire hard and low past Godden for the equaliser.

With away goals counting double, Albion knew they were out as there would no longer be the need for extra time. It was a sad night at The Hawthorns, and several players, Cyrille included, slumped to their knees at the final whistle.

Manager Atkinson said after the game: "We should have won… it was inexperience on the part of us all, including me. All of us are to blame. They gave Cyrille some treatment, I know that."

As for Red Star, they went on to reach the final by beating Hertha Berlin in the semis. Another German club, Borussia Moenchengladbach, however, denied them glory by winning the two-legged final 2-1 on aggregate.

16: Len Cantello Testimonial Match

CYRILLE REGIS XI 3 WEST BROMWICH ALBION XI 2

15 May 1979

The 'Daily Mail' reporter John Edwards, in his story, posted in the newspaper on 23 August 2002, wrote: "They came together for one game to honour a friend… Young men who were routinely abused because of the colour of their skin… A team of 1970s footballing pioneers who were hailed as The All Blacks."

This game was a testimonial match for the long-serving West Bromwich Albion midfielder Len Cantello. However, his committee, myself included, came up with a novel idea of marking Len's 10 years' service at the club by arranging a match between a team of entirely black footballers, captained by Cyrille, against a selected Albion XI, skipped by Len himself. Initially, it was going to be Brian Clough's XI against Albion, but sensing trouble in the media, the Nottingham Forest boss dropped out.

At the time Cyrille needed no reminding of the open and hostile reception he and two other Albion players had received before, during and after certain League games earlier in the season, especially by fans (if you can call them that) at the away games with both Manchester clubs, City and United, and neighbours Wolves.

Recalled Cyrille: "There weren't too many black players in the top flight and racist abuse from crowds was one hundred per cent. There was no 'Kick It Out or Show Racism the Red Card' or anything like that. And we were getting it big time. We were right in the middle of it, yet I never gave it a thought when someone from Len's committee suggested I put together a team of black players for his testimonial. It was Len's last appearance for the club and it was a way of attracting a few extra people into the ground to see it.

"There was nothing else behind it, and no one I asked to play in my team queried it. They all said it was a great idea – even the Albion manager big Ron Atkinson said so too."

Cyrille Regis XI: Richardson (QPR); Batson (Hodgson... both WBA), Berry (Wolves), Hazell (Wolves), Thomas (Hereford United), Benjamin (Sheffield United), Cunningham (Moses... both WBA), White (Hereford United), Regis (WBA), Crooks (Stoke City), Phillips (Hereford United).

WBA XI: Stewart; Mulligan, Robson, Tarantini (Birmingham City), Statham (Bennett), T. Brown, Cantello (Summerfield), Giles, Trewick, A. Brown (Cowdrill), Mills.

Attendance: 7.023

Besides it being Cantello's last game in an Albion shirt, it was also Paddy Mulligan's farewell appearance for the club and Laurie Cunningham's who would soon be off to Real Madrid for almost £1 million.

The frizzy-haired Argentinean World Cup winning defender Alberto Tarantini made a guest appearance for Albion while former player-manager Johnny Giles returned to his old hunting ground. Five Albion players were set to make an appearance for the Black team – Brendon Batson, young Vernon Hodgson, Remi Moses. Laurie Cunningham and Cyrille himself – while four more would later move to The Hawthorns – Ian Benjamin, Stewart Phillips, Garth Crooks and Winston White.

After a fairly even first quarter-of-an-hour or so, the game suddenly burst into life when Laurie Cunningham, with a clinical shot from fully 20 yards, gave Cyrille's team the lead in the 21st minute.

But the Albion XI responded well and after Tony Brown and David Mills had both come close to equalising, Bryan Robson matched Cunningham's effort with a booming 30-yard direct free-kick in the 37th minute to bring the scores level.

With the 'Blacks' on the back foot, Ally Brown popped up four minutes before the interval to edge the Baggies team in front, although the QPR goalkeeper Derek Richardson knew he could, and should, have done better!

Six minutes into the second-half it was 2-2 when Garth Crooks, a young striker who had just helped Stoke City gain promotion from Division Two, found space to score low past Dave Stewart.

Crooks went on to gain two FA Cup winners' medals with Tottenham Hotspur before leaving White Hart Lane for The Hawthorns in a £100,000 deal in July 1985. He would go on and score 21 goals in 49 appearances for the Baggies before switching his allegiance to Charlton Athletic in March 1987.

The Hereford United striker Stewart Phillips, who had earlier tested Stewart with a snap-shot from 15 yards, went one better in the 71st minute by scoring the winner for Cyrille's team.

Cunningham and Cyrille combined well down the right to set up Phillips who netted with smart efficiency. Soon afterwards he almost scored again but missed the target by a yard, while at the other end of the field John Trewick saw his firmly hit shot well saved by Richardson.

Johnny Giles, who was still playing for Shamrock Rovers and the Republic of Ireland, was 'Man of the Match'. And after the game he said: "It was nice to be back – I felt as if I'd never left!"

If this 'Black v White' game was probably a step too far for some people who thought it could have been divisive, there is no doubt whatsoever that it was certainly a terrific boost for football in general and Albion manager Ron Atkinson, who always had an eye for publicity remarked: "That was good, very good. Well done everyone."

Albion star Batson on the other hand, admitted: "It was a triumph which, if anything, struck a blow for multiculturalism. I remember looking round before kick-off and seeing more black and Asian faces in the crowd than we normally get for a League game."

Cyrille summed the evening up nicely: "It was a wonderful occasion and a shot in the arm for black footballers."

17: European U21 Championship

(Qualifying Group 1)
BULGARIA U21 1 ENGLAND U21 3

5 June 1979

England, under head coach/manager Dave Sexton, initially believed they were in a tough qualifying group for the 1980 European Championships, after being drawn out of the hat with Bulgaria and Denmark. But things were not as bad as first thought and in the end they qualified for the finals in by winning all four matches, finishing with a goal average of 11-2.

They defeated the Danes 2-1 in Hvidovre (Cyrille's debut for his country at this level), won the return fixture 1-0 at Watford and after this victory over Bulgaria in Pernik, they demolished the Bulgars in the return game at Leicester by 5-0, Garth Crooks scoring a hat-trick.

During this qualifying campaign which covered four games, Cyrille was accompanied in the England squad by three of his club-mates, Laurie Cunningham, Bryan Robson, Derek Statham, and before the finals got underway, two more had been added to the squad, John Deehan and Gary Owen. And then, you could also add future Baggies' stars, Luther Blissett and Garth Crooks, who were also in Sexton's party.

The England team in Bulgaria showed four changes from that which had defeated Denmark in their opening game. Cyrille and

Kevin Reeves of Norwich City were the preferred strikers, with the Albion man looking for his first international goal, having failed to find the net against the Danes.

Bulgaria: Laftschis; Balewski, Marinon, Tetschev, Dimitrov, Kotschev, Valcov, Marmkov, Mladenov, Slavkov, Milkov.

England: Bailey (Manchester United); Sansom (Arsenal), Statham (West Bromwich Albion), Williams (Southampton), Gilbert (Crystal Palace), Wright (Everton), Hoddle (Tottenham Hotspur); sub. Robson (West Bromwich Albion), Reeves (Norwich City), Deehan (Aston Villa); sub. Blissett (Watford), Owen (West Bromwich Albion), Regis (West Bromwich Albion).

Attendance: 3,929

This European U21 qualifier was played in the 8,000 capacity Minyor Stadium in Pernik and on a warm, sultry night, it was England started the better with Cyrille and Glenn Hoddle both going close early on, while the Bulgarian front man Colea Valcov tested Gary Bailey with a solid header from Georgi Slavkov's high looping cross.

Bulgaria's goalkeeper Nikola Laftschis then saved well from a Cyrille strike before Hoddle sent a free-kick a yard ort so wide.

Three goals then came in quick succession... Valcov scored for Bulgaria while Reeves up (after a smart build-up, and Cyrille (at last) found the net for England.

Leading 2-1 at half-time, England were now in control and they came out after the break full of confidence. Cyrille had the first shot at goal in the second-half and soon helped Reeves grab his second of the night as England strolled to a comfortable 3-1 victory.

In the knockout quarter-final of the Euro 21 Championships, England defeated Scotland 2-1 over two legs (the first game taking place at Cyrille's future home ground, Highfield Road, Coventry) but then lost to East Germany 3-1 in the semis, again over two legs, Cyrille playing in the return fixture in Jena. The Germans then succumbed 1-0 to the USSR in the two-legged final, played in Rostock and Moscow.

Five days after this game in Bulgaria, England's U21 side beat Sweden 2-1 in a friendly in Vasteraas and Cyrille was once again on target along with his Baggies' colleague Bryan Robson.

Three years later, in September 1982, Cyrille, as captain of the team, would score his third and final goal in an England shirt – in an excellent 4-1 U21 European Championship qualifying victory over Denmark in Hvidovre.

18: Football League Division One

CRYSTAL PALACE 2 WEST BROMWICH ALBION 2

26 January 1980

Albion, having just returned from a short break in the Persian Gulf where they had won two friendly matches, had lost four of their previous five League and Cup games, were going through a difficult patch and at the same time were conceding goals – 12 had gone past 'keeper Tony Godden in less than a month.

Manager Ron Atkinson had seen his team slip down the First Division table to 18th, while Crystal Palace, under boss Terry Venables, were lying eighth, although they too, had lost half of their previous six League matches.

Albion were without David Mills, John Trewick and Derek Statham for the re-arranged fixture at Selhurst Park, but midfielder Bryan Robson was back in the starting line-up, while Remi Moses was set to make his League debut.

Palace were missing Peter Nicholas and Terry Fenwick, but Gerry Francis and Ian Walsh were both declared fit to play.

Crystal Palace: Burridge; Hinshelwood, Sansom, Kember, Cannon, Gilbert, Murphy, Francis, (Swindlehurst), Flanagan, Walsh, Hilaire.

WBA: Godden; Batson, Statham (A. Brown), Moses, Wile, Robertson, Robson, Deehan, Regis, Owen, Barnes.

Attendance: 23,258

The young, enthusiastic Moses was in thick of the action straightaway, earning a stern ticking off from referee Allan Gunn for a crunching tackle on Steve Kember who needed lengthy treatment.

Statham set up Cyrille in the 14th minute but the striker saw his effort bounce away off an upright. That was a let for the hosts who then stunned Albion by going ahead 10 minutes later.

Goalkeeper John Burridge's long downfield clearance was chased all the way by Vince Hilaire. Moses and Statham attempted to close in on the Palace player but someone they collided with each other, leaving Hilaire clear to go on a place a low shot wide of Godden. Statham unfortunately had to limp off with a knee injury, eventually being replaced by Ally Brown, with Robson switching to left back. Statham would not figure again all season.

Ten minutes before half-time Godden saved well from Jerry Murphy and Moses was booked for another hefty challenge, this time on Hilaire, seconds before the half-time whistle.

After two close shaves, Palace should have gone 2-0 up on 64 minutes but Walsh shot wide with only Godden to beat and then after turning John Wile, Mike Flanagan failed to get past the Albion 'keeper who was certainly having a fine game.

After Cyrille had shot weakly at Burridge, Palace increased their lead on 71 minutes when Kember, moving forward, struck a fierce shot which took a slight deflection off Ally Robertson and sped past Godden.

Albion had a mountain to climb now, but they hit back immediately, and within five minutes had reduced the deficit to one. A free-kick on the left by Peter Barnes was headed hard and true past Burridge by Robertson. This was the defender's first goal of the season and his first in the League since mid-March 1978 when he equalised in a 1-1 draw at Old Trafford.

Urged on by a band of 2,000 supporters, Albion had their tails up and in their next attack, they drew level with a superb goal by Cyrille.

Collecting the ball 20 yards inside the Palace half, 'Smokin Joe' moved menacingly towards the penalty area before letting fly with a stunning right-footed drive from just outside the box. Burridge never saw it and it was good enough to earn the Baggies a point.

After the game, manager Atkinson said: "Cyrille's goal was something special" and he added that the kid Moses did "great and would be playing in the next League game against Manchester City."

Effectively, this result in South East London, turned Albion's season round.

For the record, Palace went on to finish 13th in the Division, a point and three places below Albion who, in late January, were sitting in 18th position, far too near the relegation-zone for comfort.

19: Football League Division One

WEST BROMWICH ALBION 2 TOTTENHAM HOTSPUR 1

9 February 1980

Three days before this home League game with Tottenham Hotspur, Albion's Bryan Robson made his full international debut for England in a 2-0 European Championship qualifying group victory over the Republic of Ireland at Wembley. Also in action that same evening was Robbo's former Hawthorns' team-mate Laurie Cunningham (now with Real Madrid of course) while Baggies' left-winger Peter Barnes was an unused substitute Cyrille on this occasion.

A week prior to this League fixture with Spurs, Albion had beaten Manchester City at Maine Road and were back on track after a rather disappointing run of results. Cyrille had scored a stunning individual goal against City – his third strike in successive matches - and was eager for more! Albion, though, had won only two of the previous 11 League games and had also been knocked out of the FA Cup by West Ham.

Ally Robertson suspended for the clash with Spurs, being replaced by Martyn Bennett, while former Birmingham City defender Garry Pendrey continued at left-back in place of the injured Derek Statham, and Tony Brown was named as substitute.

Future Albion player Gerry Armstrong and manager Ossie Ardiles were both named in the Londoners' team, as was Ardiles'

Argentinean colleague Ricky Villa and Glenn Hoddle who had just been replaced in the England team by Robson!

Albion had not beaten Spurs for three years… but they were ready to put that right, or rather Cyrille was!

WBA: Godden; Batson, Pendrey, Moses, Wile, Bennett, Robson, A. Brown, Regis, Owen, Barnes,

Tottenham Hotspur: Daines; Hughton, Miller, McAllister, Yorath, Naylor, Ardiles, Hoddle, Villa, Jones, Armstrong.

Attendance: 26,319

Albion, as expected, started brightly. They were quicker to the ball, attacked in numbers and pushed Spurs back a good 20-30 yards. And this early pressure paid off as early as the ninth minute.

Barnes swung over a looping corner from the left; Wile, despite being challenged by Don McAllister in the air, managed to flick the ball on to Cyrille who getting beyond Naylor, crashed a bullet of a half volley past 'keeper Barry Daines from eight yards.

"I caught the ball just right" said Cyrille after the game. "It was there to be hit and I did just that."

Six minutes later Albion almost scored again. Barnes and Gary Owen weaved a pattern before the former crossed to Ally Brown whose header missed the target by a matter of inches.

But in the 17th minute Albion had a let off when Armstrong, avoiding Bennett's challenge, smashed a right-footed shot against Tony Godden's post.

Cyrille (twice), Barnes and Brown all came close to adding a second goal for Albion while at the other end of the field, Godden saved well from Chris Jones and Villa following two rare breakaway attacks by the visitors.

Spurs started the second-half well and it was no surprise when in the 54th minute, Hoddle, aided by a strong wind in his favour, equalised with a brilliant 25-yard drive which swerved past Godden.

With the visitors growing in confidence, Villa sent in a low shot which missed Godden's right hand post by inches and soon afterwards Jones came close with a header.

After these two scares, Albion slowly but surely edged their way back into the match and in the 64th minute they regained the lead. Left-back Pendrey, up with his attackers, mishit an attempted shot at goal, but luckily the ball got caught up in the swirling wind and fell to Robson. The midfielder quickly whipped in a wicked cross from the bye-line and into the danger-zone, where Cyrille swooped to head home his second goal of the game.

Albion didn't create much after this but they did have 'keeper Godden to thank for their victory. He pulled off a stunning one handed save late on deny Hoddle as Spurs pushed for an equaliser.

20: Football League Division One

WEST BROMWICH ALBION 4 SWANSEA CITY 1

5 September 1981

This season (1981-082) saw Swansea City playing in the top flight of League football for the first time in the club's 69-year history. Managed by former Liverpool and Welsh international striker John Toshack, the Swans were sitting proudly on top of the table, having beaten Leeds United 5-1 and Brighton 2-1. In contrast, Albion – who had been without the services of Cyrille I might add – were bottom, having lost 2-1 at Manchester City and 2-0 at home to Arsenal.

It was early days, of course, and Baggies' boss Ronnie Allen didn't panic, although he did make one change from the side that had lost to the Gunners, bringing in Cyrille to lead the attack in place of John Deehan who dropped to the bench. The former Birmingham City striker Bob Latchford was in the Swans' line-up.

And for the record, Albion had last played Swansea (Town) in December 1946 (won 2-1) in a Second Division match.

WBA: Godden; Batson, Statham, Moses, Wile, Robertson, Robson, Mills, Regis, Owen, Mackenzie.

Swansea City: Davies; Robinson, Hadziabdic, Rajkovic, Irwin, Mahoney, Curtis, R. James, L. James, Charles (Attley), Latchford.

Attendance: 18,063

Albion began well but it was Swansea, through Alan Curtis, who had the first shot on goal. Cyrille then saw a tame effort saved by Welsh 'keeper Dai Davies before the big fella opened the scoring for the Baggies on 17 minutes.

Bryan Robson, after gaining possession from Jeremy Charles in midfield, slipped a shot pass to Remi Moses who quickly sent Cyrille charging through the middle of the visitors' defence to hammer home a terrific shot from 18 yards.

Albion dominated the rest of the first-half. Expensive signing David Mills went close to adding a second goal and Cyrille was only a yard or so wide with a header from Derek Statham's left-wing cross.

Early in the second-half, Leighton James forced Tony Godden into a fine diving save and Latchford shot wide before the Swans fell two behind in the 67th minute.

Gary Owen dealt with a potentially dangerous situation by whacking the ball downfield from inside his own penalty area. The ball bounced near the centre circle where Cyrille was being closely marked by Colin Irwin. But the Albion striker smartly headed the ball over the former Liverpool defender and went for goal, chased by Irwin. Cyrille held his cool, despite a late challenge from Irwin, and scored low down into the corner of Davies' net. This was a wonderful individual goal.

Two minutes later it was 3-0 when Steve Mackenzie, after playing a quick one-two with Mills which took out John Mahoney and Ante Rajkovic, smacked home his first goal for the club following his £650,000 transfer from Manchester City.

Four minutes later Cyrille completed his first-ever hat-trick at senior level. Mills held up play before steering a pass through to the big fella who beat Davies with ease from 15 yards.

Soon afterwards, Mills came close to adding a fifth before Swansea's Neil Robinson scored a consolation goal for the visitors in the 75th minute, bending a superb 30-yard shot beyond the diving Godden.

Later in the season Swansea gained revenge with a 3-1 win at The Vetch Field and they actually ended their first season in the top flight in sixth position while Albion just avoided relegated, finishing sixth from bottom, just two points clear of the drop-zone.

21: Football League Division One

BIRMINGHAM CITY 3 WEST BROMWICH ALBION 3

31 October 1981

At the time of the local derby at St Andrew's, Albion were struggling at the bottom end of the Division, having won only two of their opening 11 League games. They were also finding goals hard to come by – just nine scored so far, four in one game v. Swansea. The team, on the whole, was not performing at all well and manager Ronnie Allen had already used 20 players, giving senior debuts to Dutchman Maarten Jol (signed from FC Twente Enschede), fellow midfielders Tony Lowery and Andy King (bought from Everton) and young defender David Arthur.

On the other hand, Birmingham City, under manager Ron Saunders, who would become boss at The Hawthorns in February 1986, had won three and lost four of their first 11 matches and were sitting mid-table. Frank Worthington was proving to be their star man while two former Nottingham Forrest players, Archie Gemmill and Colin Todd were also in good form.

Birmingham City: Wealands; den Hauwe, Hawker, Curbishley, Broadhurst, Todd, Gemmill, Brocken, Evans, Worthington, Van Mierlo (Handysides).

WBA: Godden; Batson, Statham, Mills, Wile, Robertson, Jol, A. Brown, Regis, Owen, Mackenzie.

Attendance: 21,301

Eight weeks or so after scoring his first hat-trick for Albion, Cyrille went out and bagged his second in an exciting encounter against Blues.

Albion were by far the better team in the opening half hour, and only three fine saves by goalkeeper Jeff Wealands – one from Cyrille being quite outstanding – kept the home side in the game.

Then, certainly against the run of play, Blues took the lead on 32 minutes. Albion 'keeper Tony Godden failed to gather a low ground shot from Dutch winger Bud Brocken and when the ball broke free inside the penalty area, Gemmill nipped in to score.

Six minutes later the game was all square. Collecting a pass from Jol, Cyrille moved forward and fired in a low 25-yard right-footed drive which somehow Wealands allowed to squirm under his body and into the net. Cyrille didn't care one hoot – this was his 50th League goal for the Baggies.

And in Albion's next attack 'Smokin Joe' netted his 51st to put Albion in front. Gary Owen found enough space to slip the ball through the Blues' defence between Todd and Kevan Broadhurst. Brendon Batson and Cyrille found themselves free and running in on goal. The latter got there first and made no mistake with a fierce right-footed shot past Wealands.

To their credit, Blues, unbeaten at home, came fighting back and early in the second-half both Tony Evans and Gemmill had goal-bound efforts blocked by determined Albion defenders.

With less than 20 minutes remaining, Albion scored a third goal… and once again it was a mistake by Wealands that allowed Cyrille to bag his hat-trick goal. Owen sent over a left wing corner. Big John Wile jumped highest and flicked the ball straight at the Blues' 'keeper, who, under pressure it must be said from Cyrille, dropped the ball at the Albion striker's feet. He reacted quickest and found the back of the net from an acute angle.

Three-one – game over? It should have been on 76 minutes when Owen rounded Wealands but put the ball over the bar instead of under it. This was a big let off for Birmingham and, almost immediately, with Wile and Ally Robertson appealing in vain for offside, Evans raced through the centre of Albion's defence, took Gemmill's pass in his stride and made it 3-2.

The momentum was now with Blues and on 80 minutes, Ian Handysides was knocked off the ball by Godden inside the area. "Penalty," said referee Don Shaw. And up stepped Worthington to bang home the equaliser.

Mills had a late chance for Albion but, in the end, a draw was, perhaps, a fair result on a day when both goalkeepers were certainly at fault for four of the six goals, while Cyrille once again put in another excellent performance.

Unfortunately, Godden was dropped for Albion's next game against Tottenham Hotspur, bringing to an end a run of 226 consecutive appearances for the club.

22: Football League Division One

WEST BROMWICH ALBION 3
WOLVERHAMPTON WANDERERS 0

5 December 1981

Of the previous 20 League meetings between the two Midland clubs, nine had ended in draws; the Baggies had won only four of them, Wolves seven. And this was to be Cyrille's first taste of Black Country derby action. "I don't really know what to expect," he said. "My team-mates tell me that there is not usually a great deal of football played in these games. They can sometimes be dour affairs. We'll see."

After a rather disappointing start to the campaign, Albion's form had improved greatly and, in fact, despite being rocked by the departures of key midfielders Bryan Robson and Remi Moses, who had both joined Ron Atkinson at Manchester United, and Peter Barnes who had moved to Leeds United, they had lost only one of the previous six League games (2-1 at home to bogey side Stoke City).

Meanwhile, Wolves, managed by John Barnwell, had lost seven and drawn four of their 11 League games of 1981-82, but were finding goals hard to come by – only 11 scored to date, including two threes against Notts County and Birmingham. Twenty had so far been conceded.

Goalkeeper Paul Bradshaw, Andy Gray and Mel Eves, all of whom would later be associated with Albion, were in the Wolves' starting line-up.

Albion boss Ronnie Allen, who had managed Wolves from 1966-68, was able to field an unchanged team for the fifth game in a row.

WBA: Grew; Batson, Statham, T. Brown, Wile, Robertson, Jol (King), Mackenzie, Regis, Owen, Whitehead.

Wolverhampton Wanderers: Bradshaw; Palmer, Gallagher, Berry, Humphrey (Birch), Daniel, Matthews, Brazier, Gray, Richards, Eves.

Attendance: 22,378

The first 45 minutes of this, the 113th League meeting between to the two clubs, and the 157th at competitive first team level, weren't great!

Both teams created three good chances each… but Cyrille, Jol and Mackenzie for Albion and Gray (twice) and Eves for Wolves were all off target. The nearest anyone came to scoring was when Joe Gallagher's back pass almost eluded 'keeper Bradshaw.

Things improved significantly after the break, however, and it was Albion who took control as early as the 49th minute when they went in front.

Some clever play involving Jol and Mackenzie, allowed Cyrille to race into the danger-zone before firing a low shot across the damp surface beyond the diving Bradshaw.

Wolves tried to get back into the game but Messrs Wile and Robertson closed the door shut as John Richards and Eves tried to move in for the kill.

Albion continued to dominate and Bradshaw was forced into making four good saves to deny from Cyrille, Owen, Whitehead (a £100,000 capture from Bristol City) and Derek Statham, who let fly with a ferocious 25-yarder.

Wolves were now second best. They were second best in every department, seeing very little of the ball and, when they did get hold of it, the strong tackling of Albion's midfielders (and defenders) quickly destroyed their attacking ambitions.

Albion sewed up the points with two goals in the last five minutes. Owen's free-kick in the 85th minute was chested down by Ally Brown into the path of Whitehead who, from fully 20 yards, cracked a beauty past the bewildered Bradshaw.

Then on 88 minutes, Owen whipped over a left-wing corner for Cyrille to smash in number three.

Cyrille and Albion were cock-o-hoop; Wolves were finished!

Statham was outstanding down Albion's left flank and was voted 'Man of the Match' but Cyrille pushed him hard after another excellent display.

Asked what he thought of his first Black Country derby, Cyrille replied: "I enjoyed it. To me it was just another tough game of football but to score twice in such a big game was a real pleasure."

Later in the season, Derek Monaghan scored a dramatic late goal to earn Albion a 2-1 victory at Molineux to bring them their first League double over Wolves for 30 years, since 1951-52 when they won 2-1 at The Hawthorns and 4-1 at Molineux.

Tony Godden had saved an early penalty from Wayne Clarke and the defeat drove another nail into Wolves' relegation coffin – they eventually went down with Leeds United and Middlesbrough.

The attendance at this December game in 1981 of just fewer than 22,500 was the lowest for a Black Country derby at The Hawthorns since February 1964 when a crowd of 19,829 saw Albion win 3-1.

23: League Cup Semi-Final 2nd Leg

TOTTENHAM HOTSPUR 1 WEST BROMWICH ALBION 0
(Spurs won 1-0 on aggregate)

10 February 1982

After a 0-0 first leg draw at The Hawthorns which saw two players – Maarten Jol (Albion) and Tony Galvin (Spurs) sent off for a bit of 'fisty-cuffs' near the halfway line – the Baggies knew it would be tough to get a favourable result at White Hart Lane, despite having won there by 2-1 in a League game in early November.

At the time of this second leg encounter, the in-form Londoners were bang on course for a domestic Cup double, were in the quarter-finals of the European Cup-winners' Cup and were also doing very well in the First Division, having lost only three of their previous 14 matches, and manager Keith Burkinshaw's side were fresh from a resounding 6-1 home win over Wolves. Albion, meanwhile, had lost only once in six games, having beaten Nottingham Forest 2-1 four days earlier.

Baggies' boss Ronnie Allen was without Brendon Batson while Spurs was missing Argentinean star Ricky Villa, hard man Graham Roberts and striker Steve Archibald.

As for Cyrille, he had already bagged 18 goals during the season and was eager for more. He had scored in early League Cup encounters against Shrewsbury Town (1), West Ham (3) and Crystal Palace (2), but allowed Derek Statham to smash in the quarter-final winner against Aston Villa, and he also knew he could win his first full England cap against Northern Ireland in a Home International at Wembley, having been named in the squad by head coach Ron Greenwood.

On their way to the semi-final showdown, Spurs had eliminated Manchester United, Wrexham, Fulham and Nottingham Forest – and were yet to concede a goal.

Tottenham Hotspur: Clemence; Hughton, Miller, Price, Hazard, Perryman, Ardiles, Falco, Galvin, Hoddle, Crooks.

WBA: Grew; Arthur, Statham, Robertson, Wile, Bennett, Jol, Summerfield, Regis, Owen (King), Mackenzie.

Attendance: 47,241

The game itself was not a classic! There was far too much tension out on the pitch, players continually gave the ball way, tackles were mistimed and efforts on goal were few and far between.

In a rather pedestrian-style first-half, which Albion had the better of I might add, Kevin Summerfield and Cyrille both had reasonable chances, while at the other end Mark Falco and future Albion star Garth Crooks both tested Mark Grew.

After the interval, Spurs became more adventurous with future Albion boss Ossie Ardiles beginning to pull more strings in midfield, and after a couple of near misses, first by Galvin and then by Glenn Hoddle, midfielder Micky Hazard won the game for the home side, scoring from outside the penalty area with a rising shot after some slack marking by two Baggies' defenders!

Replacing the out-of-sorts Gary Owen with Andy King, Albion threw caution to the wind as the minutes ticked by and both Cyrille and Steve Mackenzie tested Ray Clemence in the Spurs goal, but the elusive equaliser never materialised.

In the end, it was another huge disappointment for Albion – their second semi-final defeat in four years. They simply hadn't turned up for their big night out in London, and after the game Cyrille admitted, "We played well in both games but we didn't get the run of the ball. It was a bitter pill to swallow. I felt sorry for our fans. I knew we could have done better, but it wasn't to be."

Six weeks after this defeat at White Hart Lane, Albion took on, and beat, Spurs 1-0 in the return League game at The Hawthorns, Cyrille scoring the winner in the second-half. It's a funny old game football!

For the record, Tottenham lost 3-1 to Liverpool in the Wembley final, but they did continue to make progress in the FA Cup (along with Albion) and also in the Cup-winners' Cup, eventually losing 2-0 on aggregate to Barcelona in the two-legged semi-final.

24: FA Cup 5th Round

WEST BROMWICH ALBION 1 NORWICH CITY 0

13 February 1982

I have included this game in Cyrille's 'Fifty Defining Fixtures' simply because of his stunning goal. It's as simple as that! It was duly voted as BBC Match of the Day's 'Goal of the Season'.

Albion had beaten Blackburn Rovers 3-2 and Gillingham 1-0 to reach the fifth round for the eighth time in 14 seasons, but three days before this encounter with Norwich City they had been knocked out in the semi-final of the League Cup, 1-0 at Tottenham. And confidence, one felt, was at a rather low ebb... or was it?

Recalled Cyrille, "We were all gutted at losing by a single goal at White Hart Lane but we were intent on getting back to winning ways against the Canaries."

With Brendon Batson ruled out, manager Ronnie Allen switched Martyn Bennett to right-back in place of David Arthur. He also brought Mickey Lewis into midfield, along with Andy King, who took over from the suspended Maarten Jol (sent off against Spurs) and replaced Kevin Summerfield with Nicky Cross.

Norwich had ex-Baggies' striker John Deehan, future wide man Mark Barham and defender Steve Walford in their line-up. And in the two previous rounds the Canaries had ousted Stoke City 1-0 and Doncaster Rovers 2-1.

WBA: Grew; Bennett, Statham, Lewis, Wile, Robertson, Cross, King, Regis, Owen, Mackenzie.

Norwich City: Woods; Symonds, Downs, McGuire, Walford, Watson, Barham (Jack), O'Neill, Deehan, Bertschin, Mendham.

Attendance: 18,867

On a sunny afternoon in the Black Country, almost 19,000 fans rolled into The Hawthorns to see, what was described in the press as, 'a general run of the mill Cup-tie.'

However, for Albion, and indeed, their supporters, who were still bemoaning that League Cup semi-final defeat in London, they knew that they needed to beat Norwich to keep their season alive. The Baggies were, in fact, languishing far too near the Division One relegation-zone for comfort, and a favourable result against the Canaries would surely reignite their campaign while at the same time, keep them on course for an appearance in a major Cup final for the first time since 1970.

To sum up… the game itself was okay, Nothing special. Both sides had chances, not too many, but Albion deserved to win as they were more attack-minded, although Mark Grew in the Baggies' goal, pulled off the best save of the match to deny Keith Bertschin.

As mentioned at the start of this report, the tie itself was decided by a single goal – a stupendous effort, cracked in by Cyrille in the first-half.

A clearing header from the Norwich defender, Steve Walford, was sent back into the visitors' half of the field by Ally Robertson. Cyrille on the edge of the centre-circle, chested the ball down, turned his marker and sped off towards the Smethwick End goal, leaving three defenders in his wake.

Taking aim, he then let fly with a stunning right-footed shot which flew past the diving Chris Woods and high into the net. It was a memorable strike – and it won the game for Albion.

Recalled Cyrille, "I controlled the ball well, was allowed to turn and nobody got in a challenge as I raced towards the penalty area. Then it was bang – the ball flew into the net. It was as a great feeling.

"I just went for it. I knew where the goal was and let fly at the right time. I'm pleased that I have it on film. It was one of those special occasions when everything went right."

Albion went on to beat Coventry City 2-0 at The Hawthorns in round six before taking on Queen's Park Rangers,

The trophy awarded to Cyrille for this explosive goal that knocked the Canaries off their FA Cup perch, still has a 'pride of place' position in the Regis' household.

25: British Championship

ENGLAND 4 NORTHERN IRELAND 0

23 February 1982

England had suffered six defeats in their previous 12 full internationals and, during that time, manager Ron Greenwood had swapped and moved his team around on a regular basis. And he continued to do so for the visit of Northern Ireland to Wembley, choosing to make nine changes to his starting line-up from the last game against Hungary in mid-November, with only midfielders Bryan Robson and Glenn Hoddle retaining their places.

Cyrille, awaiting his first full cap, was one of two substitutes who sat on the bench, but was told (quietly) that he would get a kick at some stage!

This was the 90th meeting between the two countries. England had won 69 of the previous battles, Ireland just six, their last at Wembley in May 1972 when the likes of Peter Shilton, Colin Todd and Malcolm Macdonald were just starting their senior international careers.

Right-back Jimmy Nicholl and striker Gerry Armstrong were in the Irish side, both of whom would later play for West Bromwich Albion.

England: Clemence (Tottenham Hotspur); Anderson (Nottingham Forest), Sansom (Arsenal), Wilkins (Manchester United), Watson (Norwich City), Foster (Brighton & Hove Albion), Robson

(Manchester United), T. Francis (Nottingham Forest); sub. Regis (West Bromwich Albion), Hoddle (Tottenham Hotspur), Morley (Aston Villa); sub. Woodcock (1FC Koln/Germany).

Northern Ireland: Jennings; J. Nicholl, Donaghy, C. Nicholl, J. O'Neill, Nelson, M. O'Neill (McCreery), McIlroy, Hamilton, Armstrong, Brotherston (Cochrane).

Attendance: 54,900

Goalkeeper Pat Jennings was picking the ball out of the Irish net after only 44 seconds of this British Home International, following a typical burst from midfield by the influential Bryan Robson who was amazed the amount of space allowed to him. Cyrille's former Albion team-mate finished well – as always!

For the first time in quite a while, England were experimenting with a sweeper system with Ray Wilkins playing behind the back line of the defence, but there was a lack of rhythm in their overall play despite their dream start. In fact, they may well have been pegged back if Armstrong had been more precise with his right-footed shot from 15 yards.

However, England moved up a gear after half-time and Keegan made it 2-0 in the 48th minute, following a delightful build-up involving four players, and they gradually gained supremacy and dictated play for the next half an hour at least, when Tony Morley and Trevor Francis both tested Jennings.

An industrious Wilkins eventually made it 3-0 with six minutes remaining and Hoddle put the icing on the cake with a fourth goal just 90 seconds later.

Cyrille, who came on for the limping Trevor Francis in the 65th minute for his first experience of international football, was only inches wide from celebrating his debut with a goal, but his brave diving header flew a yard wide.

The Brighton & Hove Albion defender, Steve Foster, won the first of his three England caps in an England defence that settled comfortably to the sweeper trial.

Recalling his debut day at Wembley, Cyrille said: "I was so happy that I took a photograph of me with my son Robert, who was only 18 months, with an England flag. It's still a favourite picture of mine."

A month after this encounter, England (Cyrille included) played a testimonial match against Athletic Bilbao in Spain. The big fella played okay in the 1-1 but, alas, it seemed he didn't do enough to earn a place in his country's World Cup squad for the forthcoming summer's tournament in Spain. New manager Bobby Robson (an ex-Albion player of course) preferred Paul Mariner, Trevor Francis, Tony Woodcock and Kevin Keegan as the players he hoped would do the business in front of goal. England comfortably won group 4, but then went out after two goalless draws in group B of the second round. A lack of goals proved crucial in the end. Might Cyrille have made a difference? We shall never know.

26: FA Cup Semi-Final

QUEEN'S PARK RANGERS 1 WEST BROMWICH ALBION 0

3 April 1982

After early round wins over Blackburn Rovers (3-2), Gillingham (1-0), Norwich City (1-0) and Coventry City (2-0), Albion went into their record-breaking 19th FA Cup semi-final with Second Division side Queen's Park Rangers knowing they were not favourites to make it through to Wembley!

The London club – managed by Terry Venables – had already knocked out Middlesbrough, Blackpool, Grimsby Town and Crystal Palace, and had won four of their previous seven League games.

Since losing to Spurs in the League Cup, Albion had completed nine League games, winning just one, losing three and drawing five. And Cyrille had only managed two goals.

Manager Allen knew his team was struggling and he named defender Martyn Bennett to play in front of defenders John Wile and Ally Robertson and preferred Steve Mackenzie to Gary Owen in midfield.

Some fans weren't too happy when they knew this!

QPR: Hucker; Fenwick, Gillard, Waddock, Hazell, Roeder, Currie, Flanagan, Allen, Stainrod, Micklewhite.

WBA: Grew; Batson, Statham, Zondervan, Wile, Robertson, Bennett, King (Owen), Regis, Cross, Mackenzie.

Attendance: 45,015

The Highbury pitch was hard and uneven – and over the years Albion had not done at all well on Arsenal's home ground. They had lost there by 4-1 to Preston North End in the 1937 FA Cup semi-final and since the Second World War, they had only won five of their 30 First Division League games against the Gunners, while also winning one and losing one of two in FA Cup matches.

Backed by around 21,000 supporters, Albion, with four survivors from their 1978 semi-final defeat by Ipswich, attacked the North Bank end in the first-half but they struggled for long periods against more determined opponents. In fact, the Baggies never had a clear effort on goal, whereby Rangers, fielding eight London-born players, but without the suspended John Gregory, looked the more inventive of the two sides and Clive Allen came closest to scoring with a snap shot which flew past Mark Grew's right hand post while, shortly before the interval, a right old melee involving a dozen players on the edge of, and just inside, Albion's penalty ended when Bennett smashed the ball out for a throw-in. Soon afterwards, Romeo Zondervan, playing in his first ever FA Cup tie, was booked by referee Keith Hackett for a clumsy foul on Gary Waddock.

Early in the second-half, with Rangers doing all the pressing, Simon Stainrod volleyed over and Allen sent a weak header straight at Grew. Then, just after gaining their first corner of the game, Rangers scored the decisive goal in the 73rd minute

Terry Fenwick and Bob Hazell created space on the Albion left and, when the ball was knocked back into the danger-zone, Gary Micklewhite's shot was cleared by Ally Robertson only for the ball to bounce off Allen's shin and into the net past the diving Grew.

Rangers comfortably held out as Albion searched for an equaliser that never came – and once again Highbury had proved to be their graveyard ground.

This was, of course, Albion's third defeat in a domestic Cup semi-final in four years and Cyrille said, once he had regained his composure, "We failed to show up… again."

Now the players had to pick themselves up and collect some vitally important League points or face a relegation battle! It would prove to be a struggle.

Albion had 13 games remaining – seven at home, six away – and they still had to play four of the top six teams in the Division – Ipswich Town, Liverpool, Manchester United and Swansea City.

It was going to prove a tall order and, in the end, it all came down to a last home match encounter against Leeds United – another 'Defining Fixture' in Cyrille's career.

27: Football League Division One

WEST BROMWICH ALBION 2 LEEDS UNITED 0

18 May 1982

Since their dismissal from the FA Cup, Albion lost all of their six League games in April before beating Wolves at Molineux and Notts County at Meadow Lane, either side of three more League defeats in eight days in early May.

That meant they had just two League games remaining to save themselves from relegation!

Arch-rivals Wolves and Middlesbrough were already down and out while Leeds United needed a draw at The Hawthorns to stay up. A win for Albion would see them safe but they would still have another chance to avoid disaster, away at Stoke who, at the time, were also in danger of demotion!

With key striker Frank Worthington out injured, Leeds boss chose to go with a defensive formation with a full-back, Gary Hamson, wearing the number nine shirt and ex-Birmingham City favourite Kenny Burns playing up front with ex-Albion winger Peter Barnes on the left.

With Derek Monaghan out injured, manager Ronnie Allen recalled Ally Brown to partner Cyrille in attack.

WBA: Godden; Batson, Statham, Bennett, Wile, Webb, Cowdrill, Brown, Regis, Owen, Mackenzie.

Leeds United: Lukic; Hird, Cherry, Harris, Hamson (F. Gray), E. Gray, Graham, Thomas, Burns, Connor, Barnes.

Attendance: 23,118

In front the biggest Hawthorns' League crowd of the season, Albion looked hesitant during the opening exchanges and their shooting, even from Cyrille, was way off target – Derek Statham and Gary Owen both firing wide from good positions.

On 15 minutes, Mackenzie bent the Leeds crossbar with a rasping drive from Owen's left-wing corner and soon afterwards the same player saw his terrific 20-yarder saved by Leeds' 'keeper John Lukic.

Before half-time the Albion midfielder was twice more thwarted by Lukic while Burns missed the easiest chance of the half, slicing his shot wide when well placed in front of Tony Godden's goal.

It came as a huge sigh of relief – from Albion's point of view – in the third minute of the second-half when they took the lead. Mackenzie, who was having a superb game, swept the ball out to Brown on the left. He found space and drilled over a low cross which Cyrille lunged for and just about connected, steering the ball past the despairing Lukic with the help of Eddie Gray.

The breakthrough goal certainly relaxed Albion and they started to play some excellent football as Leeds began to get somewhat infuriated, especially when Burns again, and Arthur Graham, lost possession when in prominent positions.

The goal that decided the tense contest in Albion's favour was scored by 'Man of the Match' Mackenzie three minutes from time. Cyrille slipped a lovely ball across the penalty area to Owen whose shot was beaten away by Lukic, only for Owen's former Manchester City team-mate to slot home from close range.

At this juncture, thousands of Leeds supporters behind the Smethwick End goal began to tear down the boundary fence in an effort to get the game abandoned. Thankfully, police, some on horse-back, wielding batons fought pitch battles with visiting fans who were tossing bottles, bricks and other objects at the officers. Thankfully, order was restored and, after the game, when fighting continued outside the ground for some two hours, it was subsequently revealed that 50 people had been taken to hospital, 23 Leeds supporters had been arrested and over £30,000 worth of damage had been caused inside and outside The Hawthorns.

James Jardine, Chairman of the Police Authority, said in a statement the following morning: "We may be close to the time when the question of whether or not a football match takes place will depend on whether the police consider it can be held without a major threat to public safety."

Cyrille said: "We had little sympathy for Leeds. Their fans didn't take the result in good grace… the press were scathing."

Remember, some 11 years earlier, Leeds fans ran onto the pitch and chased after the referee following Jeff Astle's controversial goal in Albion's 2-1 win at Elland Road in 1971.

For the record, Albion lost their final game of the 1981-82 season by 3-0 at Stoke, yet still finished sixth from bottom of the table, two points clear of relegated Leeds (20th). Stoke escaped on 44 points.

And Cyrille ended the campaign with a grand total of 25 goals to his name – 17 in the League. This was, and would remain, his best-ever scoring season during his entire career.

Unfortunately, Cyrille tweaked his right hamstring against Leeds and was given two weeks to prove his fitness before the England manager named his squad for the World Cup. Cyrille lined up against Iceland in Reykjavik, but went off in the second-half, replaced by Paul Goddard. He was subsequently left out of the squad, Paul Mariner of Ipswich Town getting the nod instead. This was a bitter disappointment.

28: Football League Division One

NORWICH CITY 1 WEST BROMWICH ALBION 3

25 September 1982

Norwich City boss Ken Brown received some bad news on the morning of this game at Carrow Road when the club's physiotherapist informed him that his centre-half Dave Watson (injured in the previous game against Everton) would not be able to play. With two of his second choice defenders also side-lined, Brown gambled by asking the former Albion striker John Deehan to do a man marking job on Cyrille!

That was some ask!

At the time of this First Division game at Carrow Road Albion, having earlier won three matches in a week, were lying eighth in the table; Norwich were down in 19th place, despite hammering Birmingham City 5-1.

Cyrille had missed the opening two fixtures but had scored in a 3-0 victory at Stoke and was now fully fit and eager to recapture his best form.

Like it was earlier in the season when the Canaries lost 1-0 in an FA Cup-tie at The Hawthorns, they once again, along with Deehan, had two players – Steve Walford and Mark Barham – who would both assist the Baggies in 1989.

In February 1981, Albion had won 2-0 on Norwich soil (Cyrille and Gary Owen the scorers) and, of course, were looking for a repeat performance this time round.

Norwich City: Woods; Haylock, Downs, McGuire, Walford, Deehan, Barham, O'Neill, Fashanu (Alexander), Bertschin, Mendham.

WBA: Grew; Batson, Whitehead, Zondervan, Bennett, Robertson, Jol, A. Brown, Regis, Owen, Eastoe.

Attendance: 15,130

There was not a great deal of goalmouth action during the first-half-hour. Norwich created two chances, Albion three, but all were missed. Cyrille, perhaps, had the best effort, but blazed wide when challenged by Deehan, while Peter Eastoe, evading Paul Haylock's rash tackle, fired into the side netting from a narrow angle.

Then, when least expected, the game burst into life on 38 minutes. Clive Whitehead found space down the Norwich left and, from his high swinging cross, Cyrille rose to head home with ease from eight yards.

Four minutes later, Cyrille moved in on goal again but this time he was brought down from behind by Walford inside the penalty area. Step forward Gary Owen, who had netted from the spot on the same ground 18 months earlier, but this time he completely fluffed his 12-yard kick, firing the ball six yards over the top!

Then, with half-time approaching and against the run of play, Deehan ventured upfield and headed his side level from Mick McGuire's precise free-kick.

Stunned, of course, but Albion came out for the second-half with their sleeves rolled up and immediately pushed the Canaries back.

After Eastoe and Owen had seen efforts thwarted, Cyrille edged the Baggies back in front before the hour mark. Although driven wide of the target by two defenders, Cyrille still managed to get in a shot. He certainly didn't connect with the ball as he wished but he was able to steer it wide of 'keeper Chris Woods who was rooted to his goal line.

Four minutes later it was Norwich 1 Albion 3 when Cyrille scored his second goal of the game.

Owen and Romeo Zondervan linked up smartly in centre-field and with the Norwich back-line pushing up hoping to catch Cyrille offside, Owen fed the ball over the top into space. Cyrille went after it with pace and with Deehan and Walford and others in his wake, he charged forward, rounded Woods and fired home a classic goal.

After this impressive victory, Baggies' manager Ron Wyle said: "I think on this form both Regis and Owen deserved to get into the England side."

Cyrille himself added: "I enjoyed the game. We were the better side and thoroughly deserved our victory. I felt sorry for big John Deehan – he will never make a centre-half!"

This hat-trick by Cyrille was only the 28th by an Albion player in an AWAY League game and only the 34th in all competitions on opponents' soil.

Fourteen-and-a-half years later, in February 1997, Paul Peschisolido would emulate Cyrille's feat by bagging three goals against the Canaries at Carrow Road. And this treble in East Anglia in 1982 was, of course, Cyrille's third hat-trick for Albion in a little over a year.

29: Football League Cup 2ⁿᵈ Round 2ⁿᵈ Leg

WEST BROMWICH ALBION 5 MILLWALL 1
(Albion won 5-4 on aggregate)

25 October 1983

After losing the first leg of this second round League Cup-tie by three clear goals at The Den, Albion knew they would have to be at their very best to beat a rugged and determined Millwall side, never mind score four goals without conceding at the other end.

However, confident manager Ron Wylie had maintained all along that his players were certainly good enough to overturn the three-goal deficit.

Millwall, managed by George Graham, had beaten Northampton Town 5-1 on aggregate in the first round of the competition and were just sitting above the halfway mark in the Third Division. They had already suffered a couple of heavy defeats, crashing 5-0 at Hull and 4-2 at Oxford and, therefore, it was clear that defensively they were quite vulnerable.

Albion, meanwhile, had won five and drawn two of their first 10 League games of the season, Cyrille had already netted five goals and they were ninth in the First Division.

WBA: Barron; Whitehead, Cowdrill, Zondervan, McNaught, Bennett, Lewis, Thompson, Regis, Owen (N. Cross), Perry.

Millwall: Wells; Lovell, Stride, White, Nutton, Cusack, Lownes, Neal, Bremner, Robinson (Martin), Chatterton.

Attendance: 13,311

The tie itself turned out to be a bruising affair. In fact, Lions' boss Graham slammed Albion for using strong-arm tactics but, in truth, his players were far from angels themselves! But referee Brian Stevens, from Stonehouse in Gloucestershire, did an excellent job in the middle.

The game was certainly littered with heavy tackles, some crude and robust but, in the end, Albion produced a wonderful performance, outwitting their London challengers in every department.

Albion, although on top, had to wait until the 43rd minute to break down the visitors' stubborn defence. Gary Owen chipped a wonderful pass over the Millwall defence for Garry Thompson to collect and fire past Peter Wells from 12 yards.

Unfortunately, the restart was held up for a good five minutes while police cleared around 2,000 rowdy visiting fans away from the seats at the front of the Rainbow Stand. It was very tense for a quite some time before everything settled down, off and on the pitch, as Albion took control.

Six minutes into the second-half, Cyrille headed home Barry Cowdrill's left-wing cross to make it 2-0 and, five minutes later, Owen brought the aggregate scores level by coolly slotting home a penalty after David Cusack had dragged down Thompson when the striker was about to fire the ball home.

In the 70th minute, three-nil changed to four-nil when Thompson bravely dived forward to head in Owen's measured cross from the left.

And with Millwall in total disarray, and Albion storming forward at will, a fifth goal was scored in the 77th minute when

Cyrille found the net with a rasping drive from fully 20 yards following some excellent work by the hard-working Dutch midfielder, Zondervan.

Millwall never gave up and pulled a goal back right at the death through substitute David Martin who blasted the ball home from 18 yards after Martyn Bennett had slipped following a rare attack by the visitors.

Millwall had three players booked, all in the first-half – Cusack (foul), Dean White (ungentlemanly conduct) and Steve Lownes (foul). Albion had Thompson cautioned for a reckless challenge in the 30th minute and Mickey Lewis for a foul tackle in the second.

Albion went on to beat Chelsea 1-0 at Stamford Bridge in the next round (Thompson the match winner) but went out at the next hurdle, ousted by near neighbours Aston Villa 2-1 at The Hawthorns, Cyrille scoring against his future club.

30: Football League Division One

WEST BROMWICH ALBION 2 MANCHESTER UNITED 0

31 March 1984

Ex-Baggies boss Ron Atkinson was manager of Manchester United while former Old Trafford star Johnny Giles was in charge of Albion.

At the time, United were bedded in second place in the First Division table behind Liverpool. They were unbeaten in 16 League games stretching back to early December and in their team were ex-Albion favourites Bryan Robson and Remi Moses while two more players, Graeme Hogg and Arthur Albiston would later assist the Baggies.

Albion, unbeaten in three, were languishing down in 17th place. They had not been playing well but had improved in March after a run of six winless games from late January.

Giles, who had returned to The Hawthorns in mid-February, had made two significant signings, bringing in midfielders Steve Hunt from Coventry City and Tony Grealish from Brighton & Hove Albion for a combined fee of £160,000. They had certainly added something 'extra' to the Baggies' engine room and one player in particular, Cyrille, had certainly benefited from their arrival.

WBA: Barron; Whitehead, Statham, Hunt, McNaught, Bennett, Grealish, Thompson, Regis, Mackenzie, Morley

Manchester United: Bailey; Duxbury, Albiston, Wilkins, Moran, Hogg, Robson, Moses, Graham, Stapleton, Whiteside.

Attendance: 28,104

In front of the biggest Hawthorns' crowd of the season, Albion looked positive from the off and, with Derek Statham and Tony Morley causing a few problems down United's right, the Baggies certainly had the better of the opening exchanges.

Bryan Robson, after gaining possession halfway inside Albion's half, had the first chance of the game but his shot flew yards over the bar at the Smethwick End of the ground and when an opening fell to the Baggies, Morley and Garry Thompson failed to make contact with the ball inside the penalty area.

In the 39th minute – soon after Hunt had a good shout for a penalty waved aside – a fast, direct movement down the left between Statham and Morley resulted with the latter getting inside the danger zone.

United failed to clear, Morley cleverly flicked the ball out to the right side of the penalty area where Steve Mackenzie, taking it in his stride, gleefully smashed it, hard and low, across Gary Bailey and into the bottom corner of the net.

It was no more than Albion deserved and soon afterwards Cyrille came close to adding a second when Kevin Moran failed to intercept a pass from Hunt.

Early in the second-half, Cyrille, Thompson and Morley all threatened the United goal while, at the other end, Norman Whiteside and Frank Stapleton should have done better when two Albion defenders hesitated following a free-kick from Robson.

Searching for an equaliser, United began to leave gaps at the back and after Whiteside had scraped the crossbar, and Albiston had almost conceded an own goal at the other end of the field, Albion hit them hard with an excellent second goal in the 77th minute.

Statham broke up an attack and moved the ball forward to Morley who took a return pass from the Albion left-back and set off down the left-wing. He sent over a tempting cross and when the dangerous Thompson challenged Bailey, the ball broke to Cyrille who was there, in the right spot, to knock it over the line.

Atkinson praised Albion's gutsy display and said that Statham and Morley were the game's outstanding players. Giles in reply said: "We wanted it more than United. Cyrille was always a threat and out wing play was very good. I am pleased."

United eventually finished fourth in the table this season (behind Liverpool, Southampton and Nottingham Forest) while Albion ended up sixth from bottom, three points clear of disaster!

Cyrille ended the campaign with 13 goals to his name; Thompson bagged 17, while 12 other players also figured on the score-sheet.

He played in seven of the first eight League games at the start of the 1984-85 season, scoring his last Albion goal in a 4-0 home win over Luton Town. And then it was, "Cheerio everyone, I'm off to Coventry City," sold by manager Johnny Giles for just a quarter-of-a-million pounds!

31: Football League Division One

13 October 1984

Signed from West Bromwich Albion for £250,000 three days earlier, Cyrille was selected to make his debut for Coventry City against Newcastle United in the tenth League game of the season.

Also in City's front-line against the Magpies was Peter Barnes, recruited from Leeds United, who had been at The Hawthorns with Cyrille for two years, 1979-81. Another ex-Baggie, Dutchman Maarten Jol, was also at Highfield Road, along with the former Wolves midfielder Kenny Hibbitt, striker Bob Latchford, once of Birmingham City and Everton and the ex-Luton Town right-back Kirk Stephens.

At the time of this League encounter, the Sky Blues were sitting 20th in the First Division table, having won only twice, against Leicester City and Watford, both at home. They had mustered just eight points and had scored even less goals, six! And, of course, they were still smarting from an embarrassing 3-0 mid-week home League Cup defeat by Third Division Walsall.

Newcastle, managed at the time by 1966 World Cup winner Jack Charlton OBE, had made a decent start to the campaign. They were in seventh position, having won four of their first nine games. In their ranks were ex-West Brom reserve John Anderson, 300 appearance man Glenn Roeder, former Manchester United star

David McCreery and future England internationals Chris Waddle and Peter Beardsley. Waddle, in fact, had been on schoolboy forms with Coventry.

Before kick-off, match referee Malcolm Heath had praised the ground staff for getting the Highfield Road pitch fit to play on following vandalism the previous night.

Coventry City: Ogrizovic; Stephens, Adams, Butterworth, Peake, Bennett, Hibbitt, Gynn, Regis, Gibson, Barnes.

Newcastle United: Carr; Brown, Anderson, Roeder, Saunders, McDonald, Heard, Wharton, McCreery, Waddle, Beardsley.

Attendance: 14,091

Unfortunately, the attendance at Highfield Road for Cyrille's debut for City was 1,000 fewer than the crowd for his first ever game for West Brom seven years earlier. Nevertheless, he was given a hearty welcome when he took the field for the first time wearing a Sky Blue shirt.

Malcolm Brown's early tackle on Cyrille prevented the striker from making a dream start with his new club and on five minutes Kevin Carr, in the Newcastle goal, parried another effort from the big striker. Then Cyrille fed Terry Gibson whose shot was saved by Carr.

A foul by Ian Butterworth on Beardsley led to an early free-kick, but the Newcastle star's shot was deflected wide by one of his own players.

Neil McDonald then had a decent effort saved by Steve Ogrizovic as Newcastle continued to dominate.

City, though, should have gone ahead on 24 minutes when a mistake by Kenny Wharton allowed Gibson a straight run on goal but he didn't hit his shot hard enough and Anderson got back to clear.

Cyrille, Gibson (twice) and Hibbitt all had half chances before half-time, likewise three Newcastle players, namely Beardsley, McDonald (again) and Wharton, while the latter also fired a 25-yard free-kick high over the Coventry crossbar.

City started the second-half much better and Carr had to fingertip Hibbitt's rolled effort wide of his left hand post before McDonald fired straight at Ogrizovic as Newcastle responded.

On 62 minutes, Hibbitt handled the ball inside the area and was booked for arguing. Beardsley duly stepped up to score from the spot, sending the ball high into the net to 'Oggy's' right.

One nil down, City had it all to do again. Cyrille was finding it tough up front but he did come close to equalising with a header.

Then, after some concerted pressure, the Sky Blues finally drew level with 15 minutes remaining.

Gibson was fouled 20 yards out and from the resulting free-kick, Hibbitt made up for his earlier misdemeanour, by driving the ball home past the diving Carr... thus scoring against the club for which his brother Terry used to play.

Newcastle, ending the game on top, came close to grabbing all three points as first Waddle and then Wes Saunders both saw good efforts saved by Coventry's giant goalkeeper.

After this fifth successive draw between the two clubs at Highfield Road, Cyrille admitted: "It was tough out there. I was man marked but I knew that would happen. I'm looking forward to my next game."

32: Football League Division One

COVENTRY CITY 4 EVERTON 1

26 May 1985

For the second season running Coventry had to win their final League game of the season to retain their First Division status.

They had defeated Norwich City on the last day of 1983-84 but the big difference this time round was that, unlike 12 months earlier, they had to collect a maximum nine points from their last three matches in 1984-85 to overtake the Canaries and send them down with Sunderland and Stoke City. In fact, the Sky Blues had not won three League games on the bounce since October/November 1983 and the fans were rather pessimistic. Indeed, some feared the worse after watching their team battle to earn a point from a 0-0 draw at Ipswich.

As it was the Sky Blues' players simply rolled up their sleeves, went out and did the business in the 40th and 41st matches, winning 1-0 at doomed Stoke courtesy of a later Stuart Pearce penalty (after Ian Painter had earlier missed from the spot for the Potters) and by the same score at home to Luton Town, thanks to Brian Kilcline's 84th minute free-kick.

Everton had already won the Championship by a mile from Merseyside neighbours Liverpool and effectively weren't under a great deal of pressure, whereas Coventry simply had to go out and win to stay up. Norwich had to visit sixth-placed Chelsea in their final game and obviously were underdogs but knew they too had to go out and beat the Londoners and hope that the Sky Blues lost or drew.

Coventry City: Ogrizovic, Butterworth, Pearce, Hibbitt, Kilcline, Peake, Bennett, McGrath, Regis, Gibson, Adams.

Everton: Southall; Harper, Van den Hauwe, Ratcliffe, Hughes, Richardson, Steven, Wilkinson, Sharp, Bracewell, Sheedy.

Attendance: 21,224

Everton, who had lost only once since Christmas, were without four key players – Peter Reid, Gary Stevens, Andy Gray and Derek Mountfield.

In front of a sun-drenched all-ticket crowd – the biggest turn out at Highfield Road since December 1983 – the kick-off was at 11.30am and it was joy all round for the Sky Blues as early as the fourth minute when a smart flick-on by Kilcline was headed powerfully past Neville Southall by Cyrille.

Having his best game since arriving from West Brom, 'Smokin Joe' was causing the Everton defence all sorts of problems and, in the 17th minute, he found Micky Adams with a wonderful ground pass inside full-back Alan Harper. Adams moved menacingly forward, reached the penalty area before wrong-footing 'Footballer of the Year' Southall with a strong low shot from 12 yards.

Coventry were on cloud nine but, after missing a couple of chances towards the end of the first-half, nerves began to set in when Paul Wilkinson scored for the visitors, who could easily have netted twice more before the half-time whistle sounded. And when news filtered through that Norwich and Chelsea were level at 1-1, the atmosphere inside the ground was pretty tense.

Thankfully, City came flying out of the stalls at the start of the second-half and within 90 seconds Cyrille had scored a third goal.

Terry Gibson zipped round Hughes and cracked in a shot which Southall could only parry. Big Cyrille was first to react and he got to the ball before anyone else to pop it into the net.

With the fans jumping and singing around Highfield Road, the noise increased ten-fold on 78 minutes when Gibson raced clear of a bedraggled Everton defence to fire home past Southall from the edge of the penalty area. This was the striker's 19th goal of the season.

The City players, having produced their best performance of the season (why leave it so late?) were engulfed by their supporters at the final whistle and 10 minutes later a delighted manager Don MacKay paraded his team in the director's box to the delight of the fans.

For the record, Norwich must have been gutted after winning 2-1 at Chelsea... but who cared if you supported Coventry!

After such a disappointing first season at Coventry, many fans expected Cyrille to leave Highfield Road but he stayed on and became one of the club's most popular players of all time.

33: Football League Cup 2nd Round 2nd Leg

COVENTRY CITY 7 CHESTER CITY 2

8 October 1985

The first leg of this second round League Cup had resulted in a 2-1 win for Coventry whose second-half goals came from Terry Gibson and David Bowman. Therefore, the return game at Highfield Road seemed to be a formality for the Sky Blues!

Chester, a Fourth Division side managed by Harry McNally, were lying third in the table and had lost only one of their opening 10 League games, scoring 20 goals. In the first round of the leg Cup they had knocked out Tranmere Rovers 3-1 on aggregate.

Once again, Coventry had not made the greatest of starts to a campaign. They had recorded just three League wins but had also lost four times and were down in 14th place in the First Division.

Cyrille was going through a difficult patch. He had netted just once in nine starts and in his own words said, "I'm far from happy with my performances."

Coventry City: Ogrizovic; Borrows, Downs, Bowman, Kilcline, Peake, Adams, McGrath, (Stephens), Regis, Gibson, Bennett.

Chester City: Butcher; Glenn, Lane, Speight, Greenough, Coy, Kelly, Graham, Rimmer, Murphy, Brett.

Attendance: 5,504

With ex-Wolves defender Bob Coy and former Manchester United youngster Martin Lane at the heart of their defence, Chester held out for 15 minutes or so.

Then the goals started to flow thick and fast with six flying in before the interval.

Centre-back Brian Kilcline and a hat-trick from Cyrille – the fourth of his professional career – netted for the Sky Blues, while David Murray (ex-Wigan Athletic) and a Stuart Rimmer penalty gave Chester something to shout about.

After the half-time break, Coventry eased off slightly but still managed to grab three more goals without reply – two more went to 'Man of the Match' Cyrille, who ended up with a five-timer, while the other, Coventry's seventh and final strike, was scored by Gibson.

Only two players prior to Cyrille 'going nap' against hapless Chester, had bagged five goals in a game for Coventry – Clarrie Bourton against Bournemouth in a League Division 3 (S) game in October 1931 and Arthur Bacon versus Gillingham, also in a Division 3 (S) encounter in December 1933.

The nine goals netted in this second leg clash with Chester in 1985, brought the total scored in seven competitive meetings between Coventry and the Sealand Road club to a healthy 26. And the result of 7-2 is the joint highest one-match aggregate score-line in a senior Cup competition any Coventry team has been involved in – the Sky Blues lost 8-1 at home Leicester City in a League Cup-tie in December 1964. Coventry also lost 11-2 away to Berwick Rangers (Worcester) in an FA Cup qualifying game in November 1901 before succumbing 10-2 at Norwich and beating Bristol City 9-0 in League Division 3 (S) games in 1930 and 1934 respectively.

And for the record, the attendance of 5,504 for this League Cup encounter with Chester, was the lowest at Highfield Road for a major competitive game since April 1955 when just 3,936 turned up to see Coventry beat Newport County 3-2 in a Third Division (South) match.

A week after the Chester fixture, 1,086 hardy fans attended the Coventry-Millwall Full Members' Cup game on 15 October 1985.

In the next round of the 1985-86 League Cup competition, the Sky Blues, after a 0-0 home draw, were beaten 4-3 in a replay by Cyrille's former club West Bromwich Albion, although he didn't return to his old hunting ground.

34: FA Cup 4th Round

MANCHESTER UNITED 0 COVENTRY CITY 1

31 January 1987

Having knocked out Bolton Wanderers in the 3rd round of the FA Cup, Coventry City were drawn away at Manchester United in round four. Having won the trophy in 1983 and 1985, United, with manager Alex Ferguson now in charge, were favourites to progress at the Sky Blues' expense, especially after arch-rivals beating Manchester City 1-0 in the previous round.

At the time of this Old Trafford fixture, Coventry were lying eighth in the First Division table while United, having a poor season overall, were four places below them in 13th but had lost only two of the last 11 competitive games and were fresh from a 2-0 home League win over the leaders, Arsenal.

Cyrille had played against United 14 times as an Albion striker, scoring seven goals, including two at Old Trafford. He was in reasonably good form, having bagged four goals for the Sky Blues since early December, and was looking forward to another tough game. "Every time I have played against United, I have been closely marked and have got a bit of a kicking, but that's part and parcel of being a striker, and I'm looking forward to another battle with Kevin Moran."

This would be the 53rd meeting between United and City at competitive level and the sixth in the FA Cup, with United having *won four of them with one draw. The sixth clash, in January 1985, resulted in a 2-1 win for United on their way to the final. And, in fact, the last time City won at Old Trafford was in that very same month, January 1985, when Terry Gibson scored in a 1-0 victory. He would later join United and was set to play in this Cup-tie against the Sky Blues.*

Also in City's winning team in 1985 were Steve Ogrizovic, Brian Kilcline, Trevor Peake, Cyrille and Lloyd McGrath.

Manchester United: Turner; Sivebaek, Duxbury, Garton, Moran, Blackmore (P. McGrath), Whiteside, Strachan, Stapleton (Davenport), Gibson, Olsen.

Coventry City: Ogrizovic; Borrows, Downs, Emerson, Kilcline, Peake, L. McGrath, Phillips, Pickering, Houchen, Regis.

Attendance: 49,082

As it happened, there would be no glory for Alex Ferguson in this, his first season in charge at Old Trafford. After overcoming local rivals Manchester City in the third round, United were hoping to do well in the FA Cup, having been ousted from the League Cup by Southampton. But they were defeated 1-0, and rightly so, by a resilient City side, skippered from the back by the brilliant Brian Kilcline. Keith Houchen's first-half goal decided what was, effectively, a tight encounter, played on a soggy pitch, devoid of grass in several places and in front of almost 50,000 fans.

Future Sky Blues boss Gordon Strachan, along with the aforementioned ex-Coventry forward Gibson lined up for United, who with home advantage, started the better, but Ogrizovic was hardly troubled in the City goal during the first quarter of the game.

Indeed, Cyrille and Houchen both had half-chances at the opposite end of the field while a free-kick from Salford-born Dean

Emerson (an ardent United supporter as a lad) was comfortably saved by former Sunderland 'keeper Chris Turner.

City took the lead in the 20th minute. A long ball found Cyrille near the left side of the United penalty area. He held off Kevin Moran's challenge and when Nick Pickering delivered a low cross, and despite three defenders around him, 'Houch' got to the ball first, had two attempts at scoring before blasting his third effort high into the roof of the net from a foot out!

United responded but Gibson failed to get any sort of purchase on a cross from the right when less than six yards from goal, and after Norman Whiteside and Gibson had been involved in a slanging match, the latter had a 'goal' ruled out because the ball had already crossed the bye-line.

In the second-half, Houchen should have made it 2-0 to City but shot straight at United's keeper Turner soon after the Reds had been denied a penalty by referee Ray Lewis for a possible hand ball by Lloyd McGrath.

Some resolute defending by City thwarted United's wayward attacks as the game drew to a close and, in fact, right at the end of the action, Cyrille tried a shot from 30 yards... perhaps just to waste a bit of time.

As the final whistle sounded, thousands of travelling City supporters celebrated in style behind the goal where Houchen had scored the decisive and match-winning goal.

While the struggling Red Devils would have to wait another three seasons to win the FA Cup again, Coventry, of course, were set to continue making terrific progress in the competition.

35: FA Cup 6th Round

SHEFFIELD WEDNESDAY 1 COVENTRY CITY 3

14 March 1987

This was only Coventry's fifth appearance in the quarter-finals of the FA Cup and they took 15,000 fans with them to fill the Leppings Lane end of the Hillsborough ground.

In fact, the last time the Sky Blues reached the last eight of the competition was in 1982 when a certain striker named Cyrille Regis knocked them out playing for West Brom!

Although Wednesday were unbeaten at home in 23 Cup ties (their last defeat coming in 1973) City went into this 6th round tie full of confidence, having won their previous four competitive games including a 1-0 home League victory over the Owls and a 5th round FA Cup triumph at Stoke.

Wednesday, managed by Howard Wilkinson, had seen off Derby County, Chester City and West Ham United in rounds 3, 4 and 5, and were in 15th position in the First Division table, and without a win in 10 League matches. During this spell they had been battered 6-1 at Leicester and had only managed four goals in 900 plus minutes of action.

Sheffield Wednesday: Hodge; Sterland (Morris), Snodin, Smith, Madden, N. Worthington, Marwood, Megson, Chapman, Bradshaw (Hirst), Shelton.

Coventry City: Ogrizovic; Borrows, Downs, McGrath (Sedgley), Kilcline, Peake, Bennett, Phillips, Regis, Houchen, Pickering.

Attendance: 48,005

Despite there being a tremendous atmosphere inside the ground, the early stages of the match lacked the passion, and even tension, which one normally associated with Cup-ties.

Wednesday started better but, slowly but surely, the Sky Blues got into a rhythm and after a quarter-of-an-hour looked to be in charge, especially in midfield.

Just after he had almost got on the end of a low cross from the right, Cyrille put City in front with a stupendous goal on 17 minutes. Lloyd McGrath won a 50-50 tackle in the middle of the pitch. He passed the ball forward to big Cyrille who laid it off to Dave Bennett. He spun away, cleverly rode Lawrie Madden's challenge and delivered an inch-perfect through ball to Cyrille who, completely clear, went on to smash a right-footed shot hard and low past Martin Hodge.

It was all City for the next 10 minutes or so. McGrath almost connected with David Phillips' long through ball and Houchen, by-passing defender Mark Smith, headed a yard wide.

With the game being played at a 100mph pace, Steve Ogrizovic saved brilliantly from Gary Shelton and, just before the interval, Greg Downs was fortunate to get away with a weak back-pass as Lee Chapman moved in unnoticed.

The tempo of the game didn't decrease as the second-half rolled on and when Glyn Snodin missed his tackle, Bennett just failed to get in his cross to the waiting Houchen.

On 67 minutes, Wednesday equalised. Hodge's long clearance was flicked on by Chapman to Gary Megson who went on to score with ease. For the next 10 minutes City were under pressure but with Kilcline and Peake outstanding, they weathered the storm and delivered the perfect counter-attack.

In the 78th minute, Bennett, in his own half of the field, drilled a long ball down Wednesday's left. Cyrille let it run onto the unmarked Houchen, who fired home off the hapless Smith. City were in the driving seat; their fans were jumping with joy and, five minutes later, they were almost delirious when Houchen scored again.

Bennett sent a long ball down the middle of Wednesday's defence. Nigel Worthington missed his header and Houchen pounced to shoot into the far corner of Hodge's net.

Late on, Shelton missed Ogrizovic's far post by inches and Megson fired over as Wednesday tried in vain to rescue the tie, and when referee Alan Gunn sounded the final whistle, everyone associated with Coventry City Football Club simply went ballistic. The club had reached its first FA Cup semi-final in 103 years of trying. After things had died down (they never did really), big 'Oggy' in goal, Downs, Kilcline, Bennett and Cyrille were all praised by manager George Curtis for their superb performances while the two goals scored by 'Roy of the Rovers' Houchen still live in the memories of all Sky Blue supporters to this day.

Next up… a return visit to Hillsborough for a semi-final showdown with Leeds United.

36: FA Cup Semi-Final

COVENTRY CITY 3 LEEDS UNITED 2
(after extra-time)

12 April 1987

As a twice losing FA Cup semi-finalist with West Bromwich Albion, as well as suffering League Cup disappointment as well, Cyrille certainly didn't want to 'fall at the last hurdle' again!

Coventry City had battled hard and long to make it through to the last four of the competition and although some of the bookies' made the Sky Blues second favourites against Division Two side Leeds United, the players, Cyrille included, believed they could make it through to Wembley.

In a hotel near Hillsborough, where the team stayed before the game, Cyrille recalled: "There was a positive atmosphere, and if we were nervous, we didn't show it."

Leeds, managed by Billy Bremner, were lying seventh in the Second Division at the time of this semi-final.

They had only lost once in 11 League games, giving away just eight goals. This run, in fact, started immediately after they had been walloped 7-2 at Stoke!

In the Cup the Elland Road side had knocked out Telford United (on West Bromwich Albion's ground), Swindon Town, Queen's Park Rangers and Wigan Athletic in that order.

They had a settled team that included several experienced players, among them two former Aston Villa stars, goalkeeper Mervyn Day and centre-half Brendan Ormsby, as well as two ex-Coventry men in midfielder Micky Adams and left-back Bobby McDonald, although the latter was cup-tied and would not play in the semi-final.

Around 27,000 fans were inside Hillsborough to cheer on the Sky Blues… it would be a day to remember!

Coventry City: Ogrizovic; Borrows, Downs, McGrath, Kilcline, Peake, Bennett, Phillips, Regis, Houchen, Pickering (Gynn).

Leeds United: Day; Aspin, Ashurst, Ormsby, Stiles (Haddock), Adams, Sheridan, Rennie, Ritchie, Pearson (Edwards), Baird.

Attendance: 51,372

On a heavily watered pitch – unlike it was when the Sky Blues played Sheffield Wednesday just four weeks earlier – it was all Leeds for the first 10 minutes. And Steve Ogrizovic had to make one smart save to deny John Pearson. However, in the 14th minute Coventry fell behind.

A swinging cross was met by David Rennie whose header gave 'Oggy' no chance whatsoever.

The Sky Blues were stunned, yes, but they responded quickly. Unfortunately, Cyrille missed three decent chances. In fact, he did everything right but when in sight of goal, it all went wrong!

Firstly, after breezing past Jackie Ashurst he fired into the side netting. Then, soon afterwards, he smashed his shot over the top after some good work by Dave Bennett, and thirdly, he simply failed to get his head on David Phillips' superb cross.

The Sky Blues continued to dominate the game right up to the interval, but their attacks fizzled out before the penalty area and they went in a goal down. A few of the players had a tot of whiskey in the dressing room to relieve the tension.

Recalled Cyrille: "Everyone was quiet and then Lloyd McGrath started up 'Here we go, here we go'. We couldn't believe it, the quietest man of all doing this! Some of us joined in, the singing got louder and louder and then everyone linked arms, even the manager, coach George Curtis and the kit man joined in. We all started to sing at the top of our voices. It was amazing... and then we shouted let's get out there and win this game."

City were certainly revved up, yet early in the second-half Leeds had a chance to double their score but then, on the hour, Micky Gynn replaced the limping Nick Pickering and immediately Coventry looked a more effective side going forward. And in the 68th minute they were level.

The industrious Bennett chased after Ormsby down the right. The Leeds defender could have booted the ball into row Z but was robbed by the Coventry man who crossed hard and low. Lloyd McGrath missed his kick yet the ball went through to Gynn who scored inside 'keeper Day's near post.

Cyrille was first to congratulate him, hugging him and shouting, "I love you man, I love you."

The momentum was now with City and, 10 minutes later, they went in front. Gynn won the ball on the edge of the Leeds penalty area. He tried to feed a pass through to Cyrille but Ormsby was in the way. However, as the ball bounced off the red-headed defender, Keith Houchen collected it, side-stepped Day and netted with ease.

Cyrille was through on his own soon afterwards, and should have scored, but he tried one trick too many and put his shot wide.

With only seven minutes remaining and Wembley beckoning for City, Leeds introduced striker Keith Edwards and defender Peter Haddock. And it was Edwards who stunned the Sky Blues with a dramatic equaliser with virtually his first touch of the ball.

Gynn went for a tackle with his wrong foot and got rolled by Andy Ritchie who whipped in a cross from the right and with

Kevin Kilcline and Andy Peake in dreamland, Edwards headed past 'Oggy' from eight yards. The Coventry players were gutted… so, too, were the fans!

And so to extra-time, and it was Leeds who started the better but it was City who grabbed a vital third goal with just eight minutes played. Bennett was fouled out on the right. Gynn floated over the free-kick, Cyrille, despite cramp, won the ball in the air at the far post and when it dropped near the penalty spot Houchen touched it on for Bennett to toe poke home.

Leeds battled on bravely after that; Coventry defended stubbornly and, with time running out, Edwards had a good chance to level things up again, but his effort was diverted to safety by Ogrizovic.

There were no more scares and when referee Roger Milford blew the final whistle, there were joyous scenes among the huge gathering of Sky Blues supporters – and the players celebrated too.

City deserved to win and a delighted John Sillett said after the game: "We played the better football throughout. It was more incisive and that was the way I wanted it to be."

Cyrille admitted that he should have scored a hat-trick. "I was far too edgy," he said, and he held his hand up by saying that he should have been marking Rennie when he netted for Leeds.

David Miller, reporting for *The Times*, said that this was one of the best FA Cup semi-finals seen in the last 20 years – a match of rare drama and excitement.

37: FA Cup Final

COVENTRY CITY 3 TOTTENHAM HOTSPUR 2
(after extra-time)

16 May 1987

Twenty-four hours before the final, Spurs' boss David Pleat said: "They (Coventry) have some quick players – Cyrille Regis, Dave Bennett and Micky Gynn – and so do we. I think this will be a classic. It will be played in a good atmosphere – and I think it will be a friendly final."

Sky Blues head coach John Sillett commented: "This is, by far, the biggest day in the history of Coventry City football club." And, in fact, four months earlier, after winning at Stoke, Sillett said, "City's name is on the trophy."

Even 'Old Moore's Almanac' predicted that a team in blue and white stripes would win the Cup.

Spurs had got to Wembley by defeating Scunthorpe United, London neighbours Crystal Palace, Newcastle United, Wimbledon and Watford in the semi-final at Villa Park. They had scored 14 goals in those five ties and were the bookies' favourites to lift the trophy for the eighth time which would create a new record.

As for Coventry City, this was, of course, their first ever appearance in a major Cup final in the club's 104-year history. And they were going to make the most of it, there was no doubting that.

Cyrille, during one of several pre-final press interviews, met his distant cousin, sprinter John Regis, for the first time in his life. "We were photographed together as part of the Cup final publicity. It was a good story – two notable sportsmen within the same family and from the same Caribbean island. We also went on the BBC children's programme 'Blue Peter' wearing smart sky blue tracksuits and I met the band, The Specials.

"George Curtis and 'Snozz' Sillett took us on a three-day break to Bournemouth at the start of the week before the final, and then after returning to Coventry we went to a hotel in Marlow to prepare in earnest for the final itself.

"After losing 1-0 at White Hart Lane in a League game in mid-November, we then beat Spurs 4-3 in the return fixture at Highfield Road just after Christmas and that gave us confidence. We knew, deep down, we could beat them again."

Coventry City: Ogrizovic; Phillips, Downs, McGrath, Kilcline (Rodger), Peake, Bennett, Gynn, Regis, Houchen, Pickering.

Tottenham Hotspur: Clemence; Hughton (Claessen), Thomas, Hodge, Gough, Mabbutt, C. Allen, P. Allen, Waddle, Hoddle, Ardiles (Stevens).

Attendance: 97,774

Less than two minutes had been played when Spurs took the lead. Chris Waddle bamboozled Greg Downs on the right and from the winger's cross Clive Allen darted in front of Trevor Peake to head home his 49th goal of the season.

Cyrille remembered: "Most of us hadn't even touched the ball when they scored. I began to fear the worse!"

But urged on by the vast army of fans, City hit back and drew level seven minutes later. Downs crossed from the left, Keith

Houchen flicked the ball into space and in shot Dave Bennett to guide the ball past the hesitant 39-year-old Ray Clemence.

With Glenn Hoddle dictating play in midfield, and Waddle tormenting Downs at will, Spurs regained the initiative but the Sky Blues stuck in there, fighting for every ball and, in fact, they almost edged in front when Gynn charged through but his effort was smothered by Clemence.

After 40 minutes of action, Spurs scored again. An exquisite free-kick from Hoddle caught Ogrizovic in two minds and with Kilcline also uncertain, Gary Mabbutt nipped in to send the ball into the unguarded net off the Coventry skipper.

Early in the second-half, Bennett who had been relatively quiet during the first period, started to run at defenders and after some promising attacks, the Sky Blues drew level for a second time in the 63rd minute.

Ogrizovic's long clearance was nodded on by Cyrille to Bennett who made ground on the right before whipping a cross into the danger-zone. The ball by-passed Richard Gough and before the Scot could react, Houchen, who had timed his run perfectly, dived forward to head home from six yards. "As diving headers go, that was top drawer," said Cyrille.

Both sides had chances to avert extra-time, City twice coming closest, first through Gynn and then Cyrille.

At the end of 90 minutes Sillett told McGrath to get tight on Hoddle – follow him everywhere. He did just that and more!

Six minutes into extra-time, substitute Graham Rodger, on for Kilcline who should have been cautioned for the foul on Mabbutt that caused his injury, sent McGrath racing clear down the Spurs' left. He looked up and from his tempting cross, the ball struck Mabbutt's right knee, looped over Clemence and landed in the back of the net.

Not too many players score for both teams in an FA Cup final (Tommy Hutchinson had done so for Manchester City and Spurs in the 1981) but this one from Mabbutt proved crucial!

Spurs tried in vain to get back on terms but Coventry were the stronger and, in fact, they should have scored again through Gynn. Sillett was bawling and shouting from the touchline, "Keep going, keep going." Cyrille had his socks down by his ankles but he battled on like everyone else.

In the end, the rugged, determined City defence held out to win the FA Cup for the very first time – and deservedly so. And as a delighted skipper Kilcline lifted the coveted trophy, the Sky Blue song echoed around Wembley Stadium in celebration.

Summing up: Peake was outstanding – he had Clive Allen in his pocket all afternoon, apart from one minute 52 seconds… Workhorses Nick Pickering and David Phillips, deputising for the injured Brian Borrows at right-back, were quite brilliant… Cyrille and Houchen caused problems for Messrs Gough and Mabbutt all afternoon… and 'Oggy' in goal was as good as ever.

This was one of the best FA Cup finals since World War Two and City won it. Great. Even referee Neil Midgley admitted that, "This was a terrific final."

This was the first time Spurs had lost a Cup final at Wembley. As for Coventry, they returned to the stadium on 1 August to play Everton in the annual FA Charity Shield game. This time, without Cyrille in their ranks, they lost 1-0.

The Spurs' players each received £14,000 for losing the final… Cyrille and his colleagues got £2,500 each for winning!

38: 1988 European Championship Qualifier

(Group 4)
ENGLAND 8 TURKEY 0

14 October 1987

This was to be Cyrille's fifth and final appearance for the full England team. Manager Bobby Robson named him as substitute for the 1988 European Championship qualifier against Turkey at Wembley.

Six months earlier England had drawn 0-0 with the Turks in Izmir but were expected to win this return fixture comfortably, although, "Nothing would be taken for granted," said Robson. In fact, between them, his starting 11 had already amassed a total of 390 full caps, with 49 also gained by the two substitutes. Goalkeeper Peter Shilton was set to make his 93rd appearance for his country; for Cyrille's former West Brom team-mate Bryan Robson it would be his 60th England game while Terry Butcher had already collected over 50 senior caps.

Without a win in their previous four internationals, England, in fact, had not conceded a goal in their previous four group games, beating Northern Ireland 3-0 at home and 2-0 away, Yugoslavia 2-0, also at Wembley, plus that 0-0 draw in Turkey.

England: Shilton (Nottingham Forest); Stevens (Everton), Sansom (Arsenal), Steven (Glasgow Rangers); (Hoddle, Tottenham Hotspur), Adams (Arsenal), Butcher (Glasgow Rangers), Robson (Manchester United), Webb (Nottingham Forest), Beardsley

(Liverpool); sub. Regis (Coventry City), Lineker (CF Barcelona), Barnes (Liverpool).

Turkey: Çoban, Yuvakuran, Tütüneker, Kaynak (Tanju), Onal, Gültiken (Savas), Çalimbay, Sener, Uraz, Gursel, Kesar.

Attendance: 45,528

England were two goals up inside eight minutes through John Barnes and Gary Lineker. The Turks didn't know what had hit them! Gary Stevens fed Neil Webb who crossed superbly for Barnes to open the scoring and then Sansom delivered from the left for Lineker to double England's score.

Before the quarter of an hour mark had arrived, Lineker and Robson should have added further goals while 'keeper Ali Çoban saved well from Peter Beardsley.

On a saturated Wembley pitch, with England dominating, Peter Beardsley found Barnes who made it 3-0 on 28 minutes and, after Beardsley had shot wide from a good position, Shilton had to produce a fine tip-over save from Erhan Onal.

With defenders looking bemused, Lineker pounced to net England's fourth goal 90 seconds before half-time, netting at the second attempt after Robson had done the spadework.

Manager Robson brought on Glenn Hoddle for Trevor Steven at the start of the second-half and within 14 minutes, with the rain pouring down, he helped set up skipper Bryan Robson who neatly back-flicked a Neil Webb strike into the net for goal number five.

Now driving forward at will, Beardsley headed home goal number six from Hoddle's astute cross from the edge of the penalty area just past the hour mark and, with Turkey offering absolutely nothing, Lineker duly completed his fourth international hat-trick in the 71st minute after latching on to Robson's superb through ball.

Two minutes later, Cyrille entered the action and immediately laid on a chance for Barnes. The big fella then tried a header himself before Butcher sent Lineker through soon afterwards but the striker's shot went across the face of goal.

With barely two minutes remaining, the impressive Webb bagged England's eighth and final goal of a rather one-sided encounter. Starting a full international for the first time – he had come on as a second-half substitute against West Germany five weeks earlier – the midfielder completed the massacre with a rasping right-footed volley from 12 yards after some excellent work by Hoddle.

Turkey only managed two efforts on goal all evening – the second from Muhammed Gursel

Dutch referee Albert Thomas had one of the quietest evenings of his entire career!!

39: FA Cup 3rd Round

SUTTON UNITED 2 COVENTRY CITY 1

7 January 1989

Two years earlier, Coventry beat Bolton Wanderers in a 3rd round FA Cup-tie at Highfield Road… the start of a triumphant run which culminated with victory in the final at Wembley.

In January 1988, as holders of the trophy, the Sky Blues beat Torquay United in round three but then lost 1-0 at home to Watford. Not a happy day!

Then, when they were drawn against Sutton United from the GM Vauxhall Conference in the opening round of the 1988-89 competition, expectations were high within the camp that another Cup run could be on the cards.

On the back of a resounding 5-0 home win over Sheffield Wednesday – their biggest in the League since April 1982 – Coventry were in a confident mood as they travelled south to Surrey, but they had been warned that their opponents were no mugs. They had already knocked out Dagenham (4-0 away) and Aylesbury, also away by 1-0, and their compact Gander Green Lane ground, with a capacity of 8,000, was not a great place to try and play football!

The pitch was uneven and muddy. It wasn't a great surface on which to play football.

On the eve of the tie, Sutton's well-spoken manager, Barrie Williams, a poetry-quoting schoolteacher, said: "We are hard to beat at home – we will give it a good shot."

Cyrille recalled, "When we arrived at the ground, it was bitterly cold – and there was no heating in our dressing room. We simply had to get changed quickly and get on with it."

Sutton United: Roffey; Jones, Rains, Golley, Pratt, Rogers, Stephens, Dawson, Dennis, McKinnon, Hanlon.

Coventry City: Ogrizovic; Borrows, Kilcline, Peake, Phillips, Smith, Sedgley, Bennett, Smith, McGrath, Regis (Houchen), Speedie.

Attendance: 7,949

With the *Match of the Day* cameras present, and John Motson commentating, Sutton started well, but it was Coventry who had the better of the first 20 minutes during which time Cyrille and David Speedie – who had bagged a hat-trick in the recent win over Sheffield Wednesday – both tested home 'keeper Trevor Roffey.

Sutton had one chance, but as the game progressed they gained confidence and three minutes before half-time, amazingly, the hosts took the lead.

The ball was whipped in from a left-wing corner by Mickey Stephens, Nigel Golley got in front of three Coventry defenders to flick it back into the middle of the penalty area where left-back Tony Rains was there to head past Steve Ogrizovic from six yards.

After a heated dressing room debate, Coventry came out for the second time all revved up and on 52 minutes their left-back, David Phillips, drove in the equaliser.

Dave Bennett fed Steve Sedgley who, in turn, slipped the ball into the path of the over-lapping Phillips who scored with a well-driven, low right-footed shot.

Cyrille admitted in his book, *My Story*, "At this point we thought we would go on and win comfortably."

It was not to be. Sutton raised their game and pushed the Sky Blues defence back. And after a spell of intense pressure, they regained the lead in the 59th minute when Matt Hanlon converted another cross from a short right-wing corner. The sprightly Stephens took the flag kick and played it 15 yards back to Phil Dawson whose decisive cross found the unmarked Hanlon who headed home from barely two yards.

In fact, the non-League side created three more chances as Coventry seemed to struggle on the difficult pitch.

But in the last quarter of an hour it was virtually one-way traffic as the Sky Blues, attacking for their lives, created enough chances, not only to force a draw but actually enough to have won the game comfortably.

With Sutton clinging on gallantly, Cyrille fired inches wide from a good position (the ball it seemed took a very slight deflection off keeper Roffey) and both Bennett and Sedgley struck the woodwork in the same move.

But it was not to be. The minnows hung on and celebrated in style when the final whistle was sounded by referee Alf Buksh.

Cyrille said after the defeat, "When I heard the final whistle as I sat on the bench after being substituted by Keith Houchen, it was the worst sound ever. Losing to the minnows really hurt but it wasn't until I woke up next morning that I realised what had happened."

City's boss, John Sillett, didn't lay into his players after the game, saying, "This was one of those rare moments in football when the apple cart was upset and it was for a range of unusual reasons. It was just one of those days."

Sutton were knocked out – crushed really – in round four by Norwich City, who won 8-0 at Carrow Road. The Canaries went on to the semi-final where they lost to Everton at Villa Park.

Coventry recovered quickly from their 'Surrey shocker' and won three of their next five League games. They battled on well through to the end of the season, eventually finishing seventh.

For the record, the last time Coventry were knocked out of the FA Cup by a non-League side was back in 1962, when they succumbed 2-1 at home to King's Lynn in round two.

40: Football League Division One

LIVERPOOL 0 COVENTRY CITY 1

4 November 1989

After winning four of their first six League games from the start of the season, Coventry then lost three and drew two of the next five, slipping down to 12th in the League table in the process. Liverpool, meanwhile, were sitting in second place having registered six wins and three draws in the first 10 matches.

Cyrille, who was so far goalless in his nine appearances in the League, had played against Liverpool 11 times during his time with West Bromwich Albion, scoring twice, but had never found the net at Anfield. He wanted to put that right as soon as possible!

For Coventry, this game at Anfield was to be their 52nd against Liverpool in all competitions, and they had yet to win on Merseyside. The first match had taken place in 1961.

City, unchanged following their 1-1 draw at Charlton the previous week, went into the game full of confidence, with Cyrille saying: "It will be tough but I've always enjoyed playing against Liverpool."

Liverpool: Grobbelaar; Hysen, Burrows, Ablett, Whelan, Hansen, Beardsley, Houghton, Rush, Barnes, McMahon (Molby).

Coventry City: Ogrizovic; Borrows, Downs, K MacDonald, Billing, Peake, McGrath, Smith, Speedie, Regis, Drinkell.

Attendance: 36,433

The match report in *The Times* stated: 'Whether it was a brilliantly disguised scheme or bluff we may never know, but John Sillett, the Coventry manager, left Anfield with three points and a posse of press still searching the trail for clues.'

The Sky Blues had never before won a League or, indeed, Cup game at Anfield and Sillett had forewarned the Merseysiders of a 'secret plan' that would give his team victory at their 25th attempt.

But after seeing his charges win 1-0, a delighted 'Snozz' left the ground with the ace still up his sleeve or was it a joker?

Even the ardent Coventry City supporters, a handful of players, club officials and certainly journalists, who had reported on various Sky Blues' matches week in, week out could not identify Sillett's ploy.

In fact, as it was, Coventry won a hard-fought battle, courtesy of Cyrille's early second-half headed goal from a free-kick. Without doubt, they grafted throughout the entire 90 minutes, with Sillett's 4-4-2 formation working a treat. And one must not forget the performance produced by giant goalkeeper Steve Ogrizovic who was once on Liverpool 's books.

'Oggy', 6ft 4in tall and as solid as a rock, was kept busy for long periods but the dealt with everything that came his way.

He produced half a dozen excellent saves, keeping out strong efforts from John Barnes (who also missed a sitter), Peter Beardsley, Ronnie Whelan and Ray Houghton to ensure that Coventry inflicted upon Liverpool their first home defeat of the season and their third loss in four matches since Arsenal's unforgettable celebration at Afield in May.

Apart from Cyrille's decisive 47th minute header, and a splendid drive from David Speedie, who would join Liverpool in February 1991, Bruce Grobbelaar was relatively untroubled in the home goal.

After a rather disappointing first-half, certainly from Liverpool's point of view, Cyrille was in the right place at the right time to score his first goal of the campaign, running in deep to glance the ball home following a well delivered free-kick from left-back Greg Downs.

In the end Liverpool, sponsored by Candy, had the sweets taken from them like a spoilt baby. With the industrious Lloyd McGrath and Speedie, the energetic Scot, stifling the supply from Whelan and Steve McMahon in central midfield, and Cyrille grafting away like mad up front, they certainly worked overtime for this victory.

Sillett, however, maintained a cloak of secrecy as to what sort of plan – if any – he had conjured up to go out and grab all three points at Anfield.

Usually bang on time for his press conferences, Sillett, surprisingly, did not show up as anticipated, but when he did finally face the barrage of questions from reporters, Coventry's Artful Dodger replied: "Do you want me to tell the world? Do you want me to end up a pauper?"

Midfielder Kevin MacDonald, also an ex-Red like Ogrizovic, confirmed suspicions of bluff, saying "Liverpool didn't play up to their best and we rode our luck."

Anfield boss Kenny Dalglish knew why they had not been at their best saying: "If the player's attitude is not right, they cannot play."

Houghton and Beardsley were Liverpool's best players on the day. Alan Hansen, returning from injury, was unconvincing, Gary Ablett worse than that, Barnes peripheral and, but most worrying was the form of Ian Rush. He had scored twice in 13 games.

Five players who appeared in this game – Cyrille himself, plus David Burrows, and Grobbelaar of Liverpool, David Smith and Speedie, also of Coventry – were all associated with West Bromwich Albion during their respective careers.

41: Football League Cup 4th Round

COVENTRY CITY 5 NOTTINGHAM FOREST 4

28 November 1990

Prior to this 4th round encounter at Highfield Road, the three games Coventry had already played in the 1990-91 League Cup competition had produced a total of 15 goals.

The Sky Blues had defeated Bolton Wanderers 4-2 at home and 3-1 away and knocked out Hull City, also at home, by 3-0. Forest's three matches had seen nine goals scored and, therefore, everyone attending this 'Midlands' derby was anticipating a bag full of goals!!

Cyrille had scored twice in the second leg against Bolton and once against the Tigers but, surprisingly, had yet to strike in a League game.

Forest, managed by Brian Clough, had lifted the trophy on four previous occasions, in 1978, 1979, 1989 and 1990, and they had, in fact, knocked the Sky Blues out of the competition in the third round in 1989 (3-2 at The City Ground) and 2-1 in the two-legged semi-final just nine months earlier.

And for the record, the Reds had not lost a League Cup match for three years, since October 1987 when they went down 3-0 away to Manchester City. During that unbeaten run, they played 22 games, winning 15 and drawing seven, while scoring 50 goals and conceding just 18. They were the League Cup kings without a doubt.

Unfortunately, the Sky Blues were not in very good form. They were lying 16th in the First Division table, having won only three of their 14 League games although, as started earlier, they had won their three League Cup fixtures.

This was to be manager Terry Butcher's third game in charge of City and before kick-off he urged his players to, "Go out and give it their all."

Coventry City: Ogrizovic; Borrows, Edwards, Gynn, Billing, Peake, Gallacher, Speedie, Regis, Livingstone, Smith.

Nottingham Forest: Crossley; Laws, Pearce; Walker, Chattel, Hodge, Keane, Clough, Jimson, Parker.

Attendance: 16.304

This turned out to be a rip-roaring encounter, played at a terrific pace, with action at both ends of the field from start to finish. Indeed, the final score-line could well have been 10-8, 7-7 or 5-8... there were so many chances created that, at one stage during the proceedings it seemed as if both sets of defenders had gone walkabouts!

Kevin Gallacher struck the first blow, giving Coventry the lead in the 14th minute, pouncing from close range after David Specie's header had been blocked.

Barely a minute later, Cyrille delivered a superb defence-splitting pass to Gallacher who chipped the ball cleverly and decisively over Mark Crossley as he raced from his area.

With City in control, they went three-nil just before the half-hour mark through Steve Livingstone who found the net with a low shot after the ball had broken in his favour following Gallacher's forceful run at the Forest defence.

Then, amazingly, City scored a fourth goal just six minutes later. A long ball into the box was headed down by Peter Billing into the path of Gallacher who gleefully scored the first hat-trick of his career south of the border.

At this juncture, disgruntled Forest fans could be seen trudging out of the ground, and they certainly missed some tremendous action.

Clough, raging on the touchline, was suddenly stamping his feet and punching the ground in delight as his team bagged three goals in the space of nine minutes before half-time.

The manager's son, Nigel, was given the 'freedom of the park' as he reduced the deficit by one with a low right-footed shot from the edge of the penalty area. The same player then darted between Trevor Peake and Billing to crack in his second goal soon afterwards and with his next touch of the ball he completed a quick-fire treble.

People were then asking when did two players, one from each side last score first-half hat-tricks at Highfield Road.

Butcher wasn't a happy chappie in the dressing room and he certainly tore a strip off his defenders for conceding when they did, and it got worse for Coventry nine minutes into the second-half when Speedie rashly dived in on Garry Parker, who avoided the challenge and turned a shot past Ogrizovic to make it 4-4.

This was turning into a rousing Cup-tie and Cyrille had not yet had a shot at goal but he was in the thick of the action, deep inside the Forest penalty area on 62 minutes, when the Sky Blues regained the lead.

Livingstone, Cyrille and Speedie were all trying to get something on the ball, as were the Forest defenders, but when Stephen Chettle missed his clearance Livingstone struck, firing the ball into the net from eight yards.

Cyrille (73 and 84 minutes), Livingstone (86) and Micky Gynn (late on) both had chances to score again for City, likewise Clough and Nigel Jemson for Forest before Cambridge referee Roger Pawley brought the curtain down on a fantastic football match.

Both teams received a standing ovation as they left the pitch… and deservedly.

Cyrille remembered: "I was knackered at the end. We were on the go all night. It was an amazing game, one of the highest-scoring matches I had ever been involved in."

Unfortunately the Sky Blues were knocked out in the next round at home by Sheffield Wednesday who went on to beat Manchester United in the Wembley final.

NB: This was the first time Forest had conceded five goals in a competitive match for two-and-a-half years – since losing 5-0 at Liverpool in a League game in April 1988.

42: Football League Division One

SHEFFIELD WEDNESDAY 2 ASTON VILLA 3

17 August 1991

After a disappointing 1990-91 season under the erudite and capable but hardly-suited-to-English-football manager Dr Jozef Venglos, Aston Villa replaced the former Czech Republic head coach with one Ronald Ernest Atkinson.

'Big Ron' as he was known throughout the game by players and fans alike, moved into the Villa Park seat after abruptly resigning as Sheffield Wednesday's boss, much to the disgust of the Owls' supporters.

Straightaway Atkinson quickly boosted his squad by making Cyrille his first signing, on a free transfer from Coventry City. He also recruited goalkeeper Les Sealey from Manchester United, also on a free, and quickly added another striker to his list by bringing in Dalian Atkinson from Sheffield Wednesday for £1.6 million; two midfielders, Paul Mortimer from Charlton Athletic for £350,000 and Kevin Richardson from the Spanish club Real Sociedad for £450,000; and four defenders, Dariusz Kubicki from Legia Warsaw for £200,000, Ugo Ehiogu from West Bromwich Albion for an initial fee of just £40,000, Shaun Teale from AFC Bournemouth for £300,000 and Steve Staunton from Liverpool for £1.1 million.

Only five players who had started Venglos's last game in charge of Villa, against Chelsea at home on 11 May, were named in the first one chosen by Atkinson – Nigel Spink, Paul McGrath, Derek Mountfield, Gordon Cowans and Dwight Yorke.

And so, by sheer coincidence, where else would the fixture-computer send Aston Villa for their opening League game of the new season... to Hillsborough of course – where else?

Cyrille was named up front alongside Dalian Atkinson – and both players were ready to make their Villa debuts in style!

Ex-Birmingham City star Trevor Francis had taken over as player-manager of Wednesday and he named himself on the subs' bench.

Sheffield Wednesday: Woods; Nilsson, King, Palmer, Pearson, Warhurst, Wilson, Sheridan (Harkes), Hirst, Williams (Francis), N. Worthington.

Aston Villa: Spink; Mountfield, Staunton, Teale, McGrath, Mortimer, Richardson, Cowans, Yorke, Regis, Atkinson (Penrice).

Attendance: 36,749

In bright sunshine, and as expected, Atkinson emerged from the tunnel at Hillsborough to a witheringly hostile reception from the Owls' fans and they were absolutely delighted when, after only three minutes, Carlton Palmer won the ball 20 yards inside the Villa half. David Hirst who had netted 32 goals the previous season, moved it forward before clipping the ball left-footed, over the head and outstretched arms of goalkeeper Spink to put the home side in front.

And the Hillsborough faithful liked it even more when Hirst slipped a pass through to Danny Wilson who struck a low shot into Spink's net to make it 2-0 after 36 minutes.

"Judas, Judas, what's the score?" shouted the Wednesday fans and their appreciation would have known no bounds had Carlton

Palmer made it three. But the former Albion midfielder missed an easy chance. And it proved costly!

Villa were atrociously bad during the first 40 minutes – they looked like a team of strangers – but three minutes before the interval they were given a lifeline when home 'keeper Chris Woods flapped at Cowans' left-wing corner and Cyrille dived forward to head home.

Whatever 'Big Ron' and his side-kick Andy Gray said to his players in the dressing room at half-time worked wonders!

Villa were simply unrecognisable after the break and in the 51st minute, Cyrille fed in Paul Mortimer whose well-struck shot was turned aside by the diving Woods but the ball fell to Atkinson in the inside-left channel, who clipped in the equaliser from a tight angle.

The packed Spion Kop at Hillsborough was silenced but there was more misery in store for the hosts.

Villa were now by far the better side, with Mortimer sparkling down the left and Cowans pulling the strings in midfield.

Half-chances were created and missed by Cyrille, Atkinson and Richardson, while future Villa and Albion full-back Phil King twice hacked the ball clear from inside his own six-yard box and Nigel Pearson got in the way of another pile-driver from Cyrille. At the other end of the field, Spink dived down well to save from the dangerous Hirst.

But then, with just five minutes remaining – and soon after Yorke had, what looked like, a seemingly good goal ruled out for offside after referee Roger Milford had consulted his linesman – the impressive Yorke found Atkinson in space. He sprinted down the Wednesday right, zipped past the floundering Roland Nilsson and crossed perfectly for the over-lapping Staunton, of all people, to arrive on the penalty spot to crack home the winner, left-footed, to the unconfined joy of Villa's fans in the Leppings Lane/West End of the ground.

'Big Ron's £4 million spending paid off in spectacular style with three of his six debutants on the scoresheet' wrote the *Birmingham Mail* reporter, who added, 'If the three points were not enough, Villa also did two things which they never managed last season – coming back from two goals behind and looking like a football team.'

It was certainly a tremendous comeback and Cyrille played his part, as always. The 'big fella' had a fine debut and after celebrating with his team-mates and, of course, with his boss, he said, "I thought we were going to get hammered at one stage. We were awful. But that goal just before half-time gave us a massive boost and once we had levelled there was no way we were going to lose the game."

Later in the season, Wednesday gained sweet revenge by winning 1-0 at Villa Park. But by this time Cowans had been replaced in midfield by Gary Parker, Sealey was in goal, Kubicki was at right-back and Tony Daley on the wing.

43: Football League Division One

TOTTENHAM HOTSPUR 2 ASTON VILLA 5

4 April 1992

Prior to this match taking place, Tottenham were sitting 18th in the First Division table, Villa were tenth. In fact, some ardent Spurs fans were looking nervously over their shoulder because their team wasn't all that far away from the dreaded drop-zone!

Spurs, under manager Peter Shreeves, had, a month earlier, lost in the semi-final of the League Cup by Nottingham Forest and they had also been defeated by the Dutch side Feyenoord in the quarter-finals of the European Cup. However, they had, meanwhile, won their last two League games, but prior to that had not tasted victory since New Year's Day (ten games back). And one suspected they were not in a good frame of mind!

Villa had done much better under Ron Atkinson's guidance. They had lost only two of their previous eight League games but there was a major concern within the team – a distinct lack of goals! In the 13 First Division matches played since 1 January, Villa had managed to score just three times, Cyrille netting twice and Steve Staunton once. On the other hand, they had only conceded eight.

Earlier in the season the teams had drawn 0-0 at Villa Park and by the same score in a 3rd round FA Cup-tie in London, before Villa edged the replay 1-0.

Ahead of this fixture at White Hart Lane, Dwight Yorke was Villa's leading scorer with 14 goals; Cyrille had netted nine and Tony Daley seven.

Cyrille, in fact, had enjoyed playing against Spurs. He had already netted nine times against them for West Brom and Coventry and would love to crack in another this time round.

Unbeaten in three games, Villa were clearly optimistic about what they might achieve against Spurs on their own patch. And, in the end, it happened to be something quite special!

Tottenham Hotspur: Walker; Bergsson, Cundy, Mabbutt, Edinburgh, Nayim, Howells, Gray, P. Allen, Durie (Walsh), Lineker.

Aston Villa: Spink; Staunton, Barrett, Teale, McGrath, Breitkreutz (Daley), Richardson, Parker, Regis, Yorke (Cox), Olney.

Attendance: 26,370

Seven goals, seven different scorers, 24 attempts, 12 near misses, eight corners and eight good saves – this was an excellent game of football. In the end it was a pity someone had to lose – but all credit to Aston Villa who played exceptionally well, especially in the second-half, on a difficult pitch… and after being two-nil down inside the first quarter of an hour.

In the first-half when both sets of defenders, at times, forgot what they had to do, four goals were shared.

Villa fell behind after just six minutes. Former Rangers player Gordon Durie, running out towards the left side of the penalty area, turned Paul McGrath inside out before crossing to the far post where Gary Lineker, alert as ever, clipped the ball home past the stranded Nigel Spink.

Unfortunately for Villa, defender Shaun Teale then knocked one past his own 'keeper for Spurs' second goal on 13 minutes, but resilient Villa hit back hard and true.

Midfielder Kevin Richardson, with a smart finish, reduced the deficit in the 20th minute and just past the half-hour mark, with Villa in control, Ian Olney equalised, driving the ball past Ian Walker with gusto!

After the interval, Spurs collapsed as Villa moved up a couple of gears, and with Richardson and Garry Parker turning the screw in midfield, and Paul McGrath, Teale and Earl Barrett doing the business at the back, the men in claret and blue went for the kill.

Dwight Yorke moved in to give Villa a 3-2 lead in the 58th minute and, with Spurs under pressure, Cyrille should have added a fourth, so too should Olney.

Spurs' attacking prowess gathered extra momentum for a while and they looked threatening for a good 15 minutes, but Spink in the Villa goal would not be beaten, pulling off fine saves to deny both Lineker and the industrious Paul Allen.

Throwing caution to the wind in an effort to grab an equaliser, Spurs began to leave huge gaps at the back which Villa exploited good and proper.

Substitute Tony Daley bagged a fourth goal with four minutes remaining and at long last, after three attempts, Cyrille got on the score-sheet with Villa's fifth with just 90 seconds left on the watch.

Right at the death, Paul Walsh missed an easy chance for the hosts.

This was Villa's biggest away win in the League for over 20 years – since beating Oldham Athletic 6-0 in a Second Division game in November 1971.

It was the first time they had netted five goals in the League since November 1989 when they whipped Everton 6-2 and as for Cyrille he, of course, took his tally of goals scored against Spurs to 10 – the most he ever netted against one specific club during his career.

44: Premier League

ASTON VILLA 2 NOTTINGHAM FOREST 1

12 December 1992

Cyrille had played in seven Premiership games for Aston Villa without scoring a goal, albeit five of his appearances were as a substitute. Nevertheless, he desperately wanted to break his duck in the 'best' League in the world and having already scored eight (some of them crackers) against Forest in the past (while playing for Albion and Coventry) why not bag another this time round!

Dalian Atkinson was missing from the Villa line-up for the first time in the season due to an injury, allowing Cyrille to start the game against Forest.

Lying third in the table at this stage in the season with eight wins and seven draws to their name from 18 fixtures, Villa were playing well, although they did suffer a 3-2 defeat at the hands of Norwich City in their previous home game. Earlier in the campaign they had beaten both Manchester United and QPR who, at the time, were seventh and third in the Division. United would eventually go on and win the title.

Forest, still under the shrewd guidance of manager Brian Clough, were struggling desperately as Christmas approached. They were right on the bottom rung of the ladder, having won only three games, while suffering 10 defeats, including 5-3 and 4-1 reverses at Oldham and Blackburn.

Cyrille's former colleague at Coventry, Stuart Pearce, was in the Forest line-up, along with future Manchester United star Roy Keane and midfielder Neil Webb, who had played alongside Cyrille in the England team in 1987.

Aston Villa: Spink; Barrett, Teale, McGrath, Staunton, Cox, Richardson, Houghton, Parker, Regis, Saunders.

Nottingham Forest: Crossley; Laws, Tiler, Chettle, Pearce, Keane, Gemmill, Webb, Black, Clough, Glover (Orlygsson).

Attendance: 29,015

Surprisingly, Forest were by far the better team during the first-half hour and deservedly led by a goal to nil, scored by Roy Keane in the ninth minute. But Villa always looked capable of producing something special and they duly equalised in the 34th minute.

Earl Barrett delivered an intelligent and well-measured through pass to Cyrille who, running clear of defenders Steve Chettle and Carl Tiler, eyed up the situation before cleverly chipping the ball over the advancing goalkeeper, Mark Crossley, who had ventured too far forward.

At the time, Villa badly needed a touch of inspiration and it arrived neatly wrapped up in mature experience.

Cyrille went close again as half-time approached and he wasn't too far away from finding the net again right at the start of the second period before Paul McGrath, up for a corner, put Villa ahead on 47 minutes with his first goal of the season.

Play was fairly even after that, although Forest did create more chances, Nigel Spink saving well from Nigel Clough (twice), Archie Gemmill and Northern Ireland international Kingsley Black, while at the other end of the field, the impressive Crossley, thwarted Cyrille, ex-Forest star Garry Parker and future Forest striker Dean Saunders.

Cyrille's first-half goal, by the way, was the only one he scored in the Premiership. He ended the 1992-93 season with a total of 13 League appearances to his name and, therefore, qualified to receive a runners-up medal as Villa finished second to Manchester United in the final table. Norwich City were third, Blackburn Rovers fourth and Queens Park Rangers fifth.

Forest were relegated in last place and almost immediately Brian Clough quit as manager after 18-and-a-half years in charge at The City Ground.

For the record, Keane had cost Forest £15,000 from the Irish club Cobh Ramblers in May 1990 and 15 years later he arrived at Villa Park, for a short-lived spell as assistant to manager Paul Lambert.

45: Football League Division One

WOLVERHAMPTON WANDERERS 3 BRISTOL CITY 1

14 August 1993

Wolves had finished midway in the Second Division table in 1992-93 – gaining 61 points, 35 fewer than champions Newcastle United, but only 12 more than relegated Brentford. They scored only 57 goals in their 46 League matches, with Steve Bull bagging 16 of them and Andy Mutch nine.

Manager Graham Turner admitted that he desperately wanted to acquire another striker, and he did just that in the close season, bringing in the former Walsall star David Kelly from Newcastle for £750,000. He also added two midfielders to his squad – Geoff Thomas, an £800,000 capture from Crystal Palace and Kevin Keen who was signed from West Ham for £650,000.

Soon afterwards he recruited Cyrille on a free transfer from Midland neighbours Aston Villa, who moved in at Molineux alongside two other ex-Villa men, Paul Birch and Derek Mountfield.

After a couple of days training with their new club-mates, Kelly and Cyrille were both given a wonderful reception from the Molineux faithful when they came out for the pre-match warm-up ahead of their debuts for Wolves against Bristol City. And the applause was even more pronounced for Cyrille when took his position on the subs' bench just a quarter of an hour later.

Bristol City, bossed by the former Ipswich Town defender Russell Osman, had finished four places below Wolves in 1992-93 and in their line-up they too had an ex-Aston Villa player in midfielder Gary Shelton.

Wolverhampton Wanderers: Stowell, Rankine, Venus, Cook, Mountfield, Blades, Birch, Thomas, Bull, Kelly (Regis), Keen.

Bristol City: Welch; Munro, Scott, Aizlewood, Shail, Hewlett, Wyatt, Shelton, Baird, Robinson, Tinnion.

Attendance: 21,052

After a superb new stand had been officially opened, Steve Bull, who was starting his eighth season with Wolves, set Molineux alight as early as the ninth minute with a glorious goal.

There seemed little danger when a long clearance by Wolves' keeper Mike Stowell bounced 25 yards inside the City half of the field. Keen got to the ball first and knocked it forward to 'Bully' who, after getting the better of Mark Shail, ran on before letting fly with a stunning drive from the edge of the penalty area which flew past Keith Welch like a rocket.

Soon afterwards, Bull released Kelly but, instead of shooting himself, the Irishman tried to pick out Keen but Welch read the situation and cleared the danger.

City hit back and, after Stowell had comfortably dived low to save a speculative 30-yard drive from Stuart Munro, Michael Wyatt drove fractionally over before Mountfield headed a dangerous cross from the same player out for a corner. Ian Baird then tried but saw his effort blocked by the resilient Mountfield.

Soon afterwards, Wolves' defender Mark Venus became the first player to receive a yellow card from Huddersfield referee Richard Poulain – booked for showing dissent when City were awarded a throw-in.

Just before the interval, Welch had to punch clear from the onrushing Kelly.

Wolves, working hard to retain their lead, withstood some early second-half pressure during which time Shelton was denied a goal by Stowell's excellent save but in the 56th minute, the visitors deservedly equalised.

Brian Tinnion sent a measured pass inside Mark Rankine to Martin Scott who, taking the ball in his stride beat Stowell with a fierce cross-shot, which may well have taken the 'keeper by surprise.

Back came Wolves and, in the 64th minute, they regained the lead. Shail fouled 'Bully' and from Paul Cook's free-kick, Welch punched the ball away from Geoff Thomas and out to Birch who quickly returned it into the danger-zone where Mountfield headed home from six yards.

To rapturous applause, Cyrille was brought on as a 77th minute substitute for Kelly while Wayne Allison and Abdul Kamara came on for City. And the former Baggies' striker was in action straightaway with a low shot which was deflected wide.

On 82 minutes, Venus collected his second yellow card and took an early bath but the 10 men of Wolves sewed up the points soon afterwards when Kevin Keen crossed to 'Bully' who turned his man before netting from eight yards.

After the game Wolves manager Turner said: "It was not a great performance but I was pleased how the supporters reacted towards Cyrille."

Cyrille subsequently made his first start in a Wolves shirt in a 1-0 defeat at Watford on 7 September and before the end of the year had made 10 senior appearances for the club but had yet to score a goal. That would soon change!

For the record, when making his debut, Cyrille became the first player ever to appear in League Football for four Midland clubs – WBA, Coventry City, Aston Villa and, of course, Wolves.

46: Football League Division One

PETERBOROUGH UNITED 0
WOLVERHAMPTON WANDERERS 1

1 January 1994

Wolves, lying in 12th position in the League table, desperately wanted to start the New Year with a win! They had won just seven of their 23 League games during the first-half of the season and had been knocked out of the League Cup in the second round.

Turner had already used 23 players and had not been happy with some of their performances. But deep down, he knew there was enough talent and experience within the squad to bring success.

Full-back Mark Rankine returned to action for the first time since late December and also back in the side was Paul Birch.

Peterborough, managed by Chris Turner, were bottom of the pile, struggling in all departments with only three wins to their name and none on the previous 10 matches, and they had scored only six goals in their last 12 fixtures.

Peterborough United: Barber; McDonald, Carter, Bradshaw, Greenman, Welsh, Adcock, Ebdon, Fulton, Charley, Brissett.

Wolverhampton Wanderers: Stowell; Rankine, Venus, Shirtliff, Edwards (Regis), Blades, Cook, Keen, Birch, Kelly, Bull.

Attendance: 10,298

With 4,000 fans behind them, Wolves started brightly enough but during the first 20 minutes it was the defenders who were generally on top. Indeed, the only worthwhile effort at goal in this period came from Posh striker Tony Adcock, whose 35th minute shot was saved low down by Mike Stowell. Wolves' first attempt came from 'Bully' who fired over from Keen's cross 10 minutes later.

It must be said that both teams were poor in a lack-lustre first 45 minutes. From Wolves' point of view, their passing was far too casual and rather sloppy. And Mark Venus was certainly lucky not to get a yellow card for a foul tackle from behind on Ken Charlery, but lenient referee Graham Pooley let him off with a stern lecture.

Things improved for the better after the break and Adcock should have scored from six yards from Marcus Ebdon's pass. And when Wolves responded, both Birch and Keen tested home goalkeeper, Fred Barber.

Wolves, who had two penalty appeals turned down – one looked a dead cert – came close to breaking the deadlock on 74 minutes when the unmarked Kelly struck a post.

However, with time fast running out, and a draw looking the obvious result, Graham Turner sent on big Cyrille in place of Paul Edwards who surprisingly joined Cyrille's old club, WBA, within a matter of days.

It was a brilliant substitution as far as Wolves were concerned!

Four minutes after the substitution had been made, and with barely 90 seconds remaining of a genuinely poor game, one end of the London Road ground erupted when Cyrille bravely dived in to meet Rankine's low cross from the right. He got his head to the ball and sent it towards the goal, and although 'keeper Barber got his hands to it, he couldn't prevent it from squirming over the line and into the net.

They had stolen all three points right at the death – thanks of course to the big fella.

Wolves went on to win three and draw two of their next six League games. Sadly, Peterborough went from bad to worse and, at the end of the season, they were relegated in last place after amassing just 17 points out of a possible 138.

47: Football League Division One

WOLVERHAMPTON WANDERERS 3 BIRMINGHAM CITY 0

22 February 1994

With only two defeats in their last 20 League games, Wolves were in pretty good form whereas their opponents, Birmingham City, were struggling at the bottom end of the table, having lost 12 of their previous 19.

Earlier in the season the teams had drawn 2-2 at St Andrew's, while in 1992-93 Wolves had completed the double over the Midland rivals, winning 4-0 away and 2-1 at Molineux.

So far this term, Cyrille had appeared in 14 League matches, starting just half of them. And he had managed only one goal – the winner at Peterborough on New Year's Day.

"I was struggling with my form. I had been used as a substitute quite a few times, once against Albion in a 3-2 defeat at The Hawthorns. It was great to be back there. It was a touching moment for me to receive the applause of both sets of fans."

Wolverhampton Wanderers: Stowell; Thompson, Venus, Masters, Blades, Shirtliff, Marsden, Ferguson, Regis (Rankine), Kelly, Keen.

Birmingham City: Bennett; Huxford, Frain, Cooper, Barnett, Dryden, Lowe, Claridge, Saville, Peschisolido (McGivern), Doherty (De Souza).

Attendance: 24,931

In swirling snow, it was lowly Blues who started this midweek evening game far better than their hosts Wolves and, early on, future Wolves striker Steve Claridge, Andy Saville and Paul Peschisolido, all came close to breaching one of the Division's outstanding and meanest defences.

Playing with a free, open style, the visitors certainly didn't look like a team in trouble at the foot of the table, but gradually Wolves sorted themselves out and got to grips with the situation, pushing Blues back into their own half of the field with a series of forceful attacks down the right flank.

In truth, the overall play during the first 44 minutes was fairly even but then, seconds before half-time, Cyrille put Wolves ahead.

David Kelly actually missed Andy Thompson's low right-wing cross as it flew into the middle of the penalty area, but Cyrille gambled, darting in front of Richard Dryden and Dave Barnett to bundle the ball home from five yards.

"To score then was something special for me – as it was my first goal for Wolves at Molineux. I believe the last time I netted there was for Albion in a 2-1 win in May 1982," recalled Cyrille.

Bennett had already saved from Kevin Keen within a minute of the restart, but soon afterwards it was 2-0 to Wolves, but there was certainly a lot of controversy surrounding David Kelly's goal.

The former Walsall striker, lurking way upfield, looked at least 15 yards offside, and that's not exaggerating, when Peter Shirtliff found Kevin Keen running across the penalty area to come face to face with Blues' 'keeper Ian Bennett, before slipping the ball sidewards for Kelly to roll it into a gaping net.

Blues were dumbfounded! Five players and assistant manager Ed Stein swarmed round referee Dermot Gallagher, and another five, plus head coach David Howell, surrounded the linesman on the touchline. The two officials, between them, upheld the decision, indicating that Kelly had not been interfering with play when Keen first received the ball.

Conceding a second goal came as a stunning blow to Blues who struggled to get back into the game as manager Barry Fry tried furiously to motivate his players from the touchline.

In the settling snow, Darren Ferguson, Cyrille, Chris Marsden and the outstanding Keen could easily have added more goals but all credit to Blues' central defenders who battled on bravely until the powerful Neil Masters, moving menacingly forward, cracked a vicious drive high on to a post, and down through the snow before bobbling into the net off Keen's legs for the third goal.

By this time, there was a degree of arrogance about Wolves. They certainly had the better of the exchanges (and decisions) in the second-half which, at times, was rather one-sided but, without doubt, Blues had played the better football before the interval.

Totally perplexed and angry at the decision that cost them a second crucial goal, the Blues' players trudged despondently off the Molineux pitch, heads bowed and staring relegation smack in the face.

Three days after this encounter with the Brummies, Cyrille – who, in fact, had just netted his last goal for Wolves – faced his former club, West Bromwich Albion, once again. And it was the Baggies who came out on top for the second time, completing the double with a 2-1 victory at Molineux. This was certainly not the result Cyrille or, indeed, his team-mates wanted!

As for Blues, their struggles continued and in the end they slipped out of the First Division and into the third tier of English football for only the second time in the club's history.

48: Football League Division Two

WYCOMBE WANDERERS 3 CAMBRIDGE UNITED 0

13 August 1994

Signed by Wycombe manager Martin O'Neill from Wolverhampton Wanderers just prior to pre-season training, Cyrille was included in the 'Chairboys' line-up for the opening game of the 1994-95 campaign alongside another former West Bromwich Albion striker, Simon Garner.

Cyrille was 'fit and rarin' to go' and every reporter available wanted to grab a few words with the former England striker ahead of the first-ever Second Division League game at Adams Park. In fact, an ardent West Brom supporter – Ron Ferriday – caught up with him an hour or so before kick-off. The Baggies were at Luton – not too far away – and on route to Kenilworth Road. Ron had dropped by to make contact with one of his heroes.

Asked how he was preparing for life with another new club, Cyrille replied, "I have always looked forward to a challenge – and this will be no different to previous ones. I love my football, always have, always will, and I aim to give it my best out on the pitch for Wycombe."

Promoted via the play-offs (they beat Preston North End 4-2 at Wembley in the Division Three final) Wycombe had nine players who had been involved in that triumph available to take on

Cambridge... those missing were Nicky Reid (another player with a WBA connection) and Steve Guppy.

Cambridge, managed by Gary Johnson, had finished tenth in Division Two in 1993-94. They had Australian John Filan in goal and the Canadian Carlo Corazzin and Efon Elad, ex-Cologne, in attack, along with the former Brentford, Maidstone United and Watford striker Steve Butler, who had netted 21 goals the previous season and almost 100 during his career.

Wycombe Wanderers: P. Hyde; Cousins, Titterton, Crossley. Evans, Ryan, Carroll, Thompson, Regis, Garner (Hemmings), Stapleton (Creaser).

Cambridge United: Filan; Hunter, Barrick, Craddock, Heathcote, O'Shea, M Hyde, Elad (Morah), Butler, Corazzin, Nyamah (Fowler).

Attendance: 5,782

It turned out to be a great start for Cyrille and, indeed, for Wycombe, who opened their first-ever Second Division campaign with a convincing 3-0 home victory over a gutsy Cambridge United side.

Veteran marksman Garner, who already had 168 League goals under his belt (168 for Blackburn), opened the scoring for Wanderers after just two minutes and 17 seconds.

David Titterton thumped a long ball into the United penalty area for Terry Evans to rise and head down for the ex-Ewood Park favourite who, without hesitation, simply blasted a right-footed rocket into the net past a bemused Filan.

United responded well but they couldn't break down a resilient Wanderers in which Matt Crossley and Terry Evans excelled.

Cyrille and Garner both had half-chances to double Wycombe's lead before half-time but Filan, and the outside of an upright, denied them accordingly.

The visitors started the second period strongly and, indeed, they had their best spell during the first 25 minutes after the break. Home 'keeper Paul Hyde had to be alert to deny Junior Hunter on 68 minutes while Butler shot over when well placed in front of goal.

Despite coming under the cosh, Wycombe got a second wind and Cyrille saw a terrific downward header thwarted by a Gordon Bank's style one-handed save from the U's 'keeper, Filan.

Wanderers forward Dave Carroll was, at this juncture, having one of those games! He should have scored at least three times, possibly four, with the two best chances coming midway through the second-half, when he struck an upright twice in quick succession, followed soon afterwards by one of his one-man mazy runs which he had produced against Preston at Wembley a few months earlier.

Thankfully, Wycombe went further ahead in the 80th minute when substitute Tony Hemmings thumped the ball home from fully 25 yards, the ball taking a slight deflection off Dean Barrick before nestling in the back of Filan's net. And then, three minutes later, Jason Cousins wrapped things up for the Wanderers when he scored from the penalty spot after Carroll had been brought down by Micah Hyde.

Speaking after the game, Wanderers manager O'Neill commented, "It could not have started any better. The first goal was a great start. We needed the second goal to basically kill the match. Cambridge had some chances.

"I heard that there was talk in the club bars last week that we were staring relegation in the face. Relegation is something we don't really think about here. We have had a good win, now we have to build." And they did, slowly but surely.

49: Football League Division Two

BIRMINGHAM CITY 0 WYCOMBE WANDERERS 1

30 August 1994

Saturday, 30 August 1994 was to be a special occasion for the Regis family in general.

Cyrille was all set to play against his kid brother, Dave, in a League game at St Andrew's for the first and only time in his professional career.

Having already played four games for the 'Chairboys' and bagged his first goal, in a 2-1 League Cup defeat at Brighton, Cyrille had yet to find the net in a Football League match and what better place to do it than against Birmingham City, the club he had already netted against before when playing for Albion and Wolves.

Cyrille's brother Dave, six years younger, made his Football League debut for Notts County in 1990, having also played for Barnet, Plymouth Argyle, Bournemouth and Stoke City before joining Blues earlier in the month.

Interesting Fact: Between them the Regis brothers scored a total of 269 goals in exactly 1,000 club appearances at senior level. Cyrille's record was, of course, 2095 strikes in 741 outings, Dave's 64 in 259.

Birmingham City: Bennett; Hiley, Scott, Ward, Whyte, Daish, Tait, Claridge, D. Regis, Dominguez (Donowa), De Souza (Saville).

Wycombe Wanderers: Hyde; Cousins, Brown, Evans, Turner, Ryan, Carroll (Hutchinson), Thompson, C. Regis, Garner, Stapleton.

Attendance: 14,305

Relegated Blues had won two and lost one of their first three League games in 1994-95; promoted Wycombe (competing in only their second season in the League) had also won two and drawn one of their opening three fixtures. Managed respectively by Barry Fry and Martin O'Neill – the latter having been in charge at Adams Park for four years – both teams had started off well and there was a good crowd inside St Andrew's to see the action.

Cyrille beat his brother by having the first shot of the game – his effort being saved comfortably low down by Ian Bennett.

Blues had more of the ball than Wycombe during the opening half hour but failed to create a worthwhile opening while at the other end of the field, Cyrille went close with a header and Bennett had to be alert to keep out a decent free-kick from the in-form Simon Garner.

The stats covering the first 45 minutes handed Blues' a slight advantage in terms of possession but Wycombe always looked threatening – especially on the break – and after Steve Claridge had missed a gilt-edged chance, the 'Chairboys' took the lead halfway through the second-half.

Cyrille, who was certainly not marked as closely as one would expect him to be given his reputation, showed immense strength as he moved in from the left with his eyes peeled on the path of substitute Simon Hutchinson's deep cross from the opposite flank. The big fella, roaring in, rose highest to plant a firm header high into the net past Ian Bennett for his first League goal for his fifth club.

It was a cracker – and it gave the 'Chairboys' that extra incentive, while at the same time it injected a massive confidence-boost into their system.

With grim determination, they managed to hold on to what they had worked for, and despite the home side dictating the play, agile goalkeeper Paul Hyde dealt with everything that came his way, while his co-defenders battled on gamely. The Wanderers duly held out to claim an excellent away victory... their first in the third tier of English football. And more would follow in due course.

As the season progressed, Blues went from strength. They moved to the top of the table on New Year's Eve (after a crushing 7-1 win over Blackpool) and remained in the top three until the season's end, winning the Championship by four points from Brentford.

As for Wycombe, they battled on well and finished a creditable sixth, missing out on the play-offs by a mere three points – one win in fact. Cyrille ended up as joint top-scorer in the League with nine goals.

50: Football League Division Three

DONCASTER ROVERS 1 CHESTER CITY 2

30 March 1996

This was to be Cyrille's last ever appearance as a professional footballer at competitive level... his 610th in the Football League/ Premiership, his 741st at club level (including 40 as a substitute) and his 754th overall.

Remember, he had made his senior debut for West Bromwich Albion in August 1977 and since that late summer evening League Cup victory over Rotherham United at The Hawthorns, he had lined up against almost 100 different clubs, scoring against 57 of them.

Chester were lying eighth in Division Three at the time of this away encounter with mid-table Doncaster Rovers at Belle Vue and, having already reached the personal milestone of 200 club goals while playing for the 'Blues', Cyrille was hoping to go out with a bang.

Doncaster Rovers: D. Williams; Ashley, Parrish, Moore, Gore, Jones, Warren, McGuire, Smith, P. Williams (Cramb), Wright.

Chester City: Stewart; Davidson, Burnham, Brien, Jackson, Whelan, Richardson (Fisher), Priest, Regis (Rimmer), Milner, Noteman (Murphy).

Attendance: 1,548

Darren 'Big Dave' Moore, who became a huge pal of Cyrille's in later years, and would play for Albion between 2001 and 2006, lined up at the heart of the Doncaster defence, while Cyrille's former Wolves team-mate Kevin Ashley and ex-Albion and Northern Ireland international Paul Williams, another loanee from Rochdale, also started the game for the hosts at right-back and centre-forward respectively.

Another former Albion player, Tony Brien, was in the Chester line-up, along with veteran defender Peter Jackson, who had already made over 600 League appearances.

Unfortunately, less than 1,550 spectators saw Cyrille's final game – Rovers' second lowest attendance of the season – and after a rather low-key first 44 minutes, when Cyrille managed two efforts on goal, it was the home side who went in front seconds before half-time when Paul Williams found the net with a rasping drive as two Chester defenders back-pedalled.

But following manager Kevin Ratcliffe's half-time team talk, Chester burst into life straight after the interval and within two minutes of the restart, Spencer Whelan headed home the equaliser from Kevin Noteman's cross.

Chester suddenly looked a different side and although goalkeeper Billy Stewart had to pull off two fine saves to deny Jermain Wright and Sean Parrish, the visitors' defence looked pretty solid.

Then City's manager, Ratcliffe, gambled by sending on all three substitutes in quick succession – Stuart Rimmer replaced the tiring Cyrille who got a decent applause as he left the field, his football career over, and John Murphy for Noteman, both in the 64th minute, followed by Neil Fisher for Nick Richardson halfway through the half. It was a gamble that paid dividends.

Immediately, Chester started to play some intelligent football, and chances were being created. The minutes ticked by and then with time fast running out, Murphy pounced to snatch an injury-time winner.

A slick, decisive movement involving Fisher and Davidson, resulted in 'Man of the Match' Chris Priest crossing hard and low into the penalty area where Murphy arrived on cue to fire home past 'keeper Dean Williams.

What a finish. This was Chester's first away win since 30 December 1995 and the three points gained moved them back up to seventh place in the table.

As for Cyrille... he ended his career with a win – just like it had started back in 1977. He bagged seven goals in 33 appearances for Chester... choosing the header from David Flitcroft's corner in a 3-2 home win over Plymouth Argyle in his third start for the club as his best.

He also picked out his three other favourite Chester goals: (a) a bullet header against Hereford United in a 2-1 League win; (b) his cracking right-footed drive into the top corner of the Leyton Orient net in a 2-0 victory at Brisbane Road and (c) his powerful shot high past 'keeper Lee Bracey in the 1-1 home draw with Bury.

After Cyrille's farewell appearance for Chester, his manager at the Deva Stadium, Kevin Ratcliffe, said, "I knew, deep down, that this would be Cyrille's farewell appearance. He had been struggling with a leg injury since late February but wanted to have one last shot, especially with 'Big Dave' marking him. He departed with pride, his head held high after a terrific career. I certainly had some tough battles with him during my Everton days. He was strong, mobile, could head a ball as hard as some players could kick one, and there is no doubt he could also shoot – some of his goals were quite stunning, as we know."

What People Have Said About Cyrille

'Losing Cyrille has left a void in my life that will never be filled' ~ *Julia (Cyrille's wife)*

'The ultimate hero, a wonderful, exciting centre-forward' ~ *John Williams (WBA Chairman, 2018)*

'Everyone loved Cyrille. I remember him scoring a goal in front of film star Bo Derek. He was asked afterwards if he would like a date with Bo or score a goal. He replied, "Score a goal." He was like Martin Luther King – always turning the other cheek. He was a truly great player'~ *Ian Wright (former Arsenal and England striker)*

'I was devastated when I heard about Cyrille's death. He was my all-time footballing hero' ~ *Dion Dublin (ex-Coventry City, Manchester United footballer)*

'His commanding physical appearance and devastating forays into the penalty area were awesome' ~ *Gary Bannister (ex-Coventry and West Brom player)*

'He was an outstanding player who handled himself with such class. I thank him for leading the way' ~ (Jermaine Jenas (ex-Spurs).

'Cyrille was the main reason why I wanted to play football. He was an inspiration to me' ~ *Andy Cole (ex-Arsenal, Blackburn Rovers, Manchester United)*

'Cyrille was a legend… and his continued work within football was highly valued' ~ *David James (West Bromwich Albion supporter, Rustenburg)*

'He was a great man and a wonderful player' ~ *Chas Sumner (Chester City)*

'He played a lion's part in City's 1987 FA Cup campaign' ~ *Jim Brown (Coventry City statistician)*

'Equally strong and powerful in the air, he developed into the complete and archetypal English centre-forward' ~ *Chris Moore (Daily Mail)*

'Cyrille helped me a lot when I was a youngster. He was a great footballing man' ~ *Gareth Bale (ex-Spurs, now Real Madrid)*

I was in awe of Cyrille when, as a 13 year-old, I attended The Hawthorns for a trial and saw him in action. He was brilliant' ~ *Alan Shearer (ex-Southampton, Blackburn and Newcastle United)*

'His power just mesmerised me; he was impossible to foul!' ~ *Adrian Chiles (BBC Radio 5)*

'He was like an ox, but in fact he was a gentle giant' ~ *Bill Howell (Evening Mail)*

'His blinding pace, physical strength and shear bravery reduced many a highly-rated defence to rubble' ~ *Hugh Jamieson (former freelance football reporter)*

'Defenders knew that Cyrille had a slow-burning fuse, but when he went off, he went off like a firecracker' ~ *Kevin Moran (Manchester United)*

'He was a terrific, all-action footballer and a great player' ~ *Bruce Grobbelaar (ex-goalkeeper)*

'Cyrille was a wonderful asset to the team; a commanding centre-forward who scored some brilliant goals. He was an awesome centre-forward with shear power' ~ *Bryan Robson (former Albion team-mate)*

'I'd never seen anyone with muscles like Cyrille – he even had them in his head' ~ *Paul Gascoigne (ex-player)*

'Just think what he would have done if only he could run' ~ *Steve Ogrizovic (Coventry City goalkeeper)*

'He was awesome at times... and I was mighty relieved to be in the same team as him rather than playing against him' ~ *John Wile (former Albion captain)*

'His tremendous physical attributes overshadowed his wonderful skill and general footballing ability' ~ *Brendon Batson (one of Albion's 'Three Degrees')*

'He was phenomenal' ~ *John Sillett (Coventry City head coach and manager)*

"I told him to go out and excite me, and he did. He is certainly up near the top of the list with regards to the best players I ever managed. A genuinely nice guy' ~ *Ron Atkinson (Cyrille's manager at The Hawthorns and Villa Park)*

'The goal Cyrille scored against Manchester City at Maine Road in April 1978 was as close to being the best I had ever seen and I've been in football since 1932' ~ *Joe Mercer (ex-Arsenal and England)*

'He was some player... I never enjoyed playing against him – he was good, very good' ~ *Alan Hansen (ex-Liverpool defender)*

'There's no doubt whatsoever, Cyrille was a true hero in football. He helped change attitudes on the terraces and in society' ~ *Jeremy Corbyn (MP, Labour leader)*

'I believe we could have won the World Cup in 1982 if Cyrille had been fit to play... I desperately wanted Ron Greenwood to take him to Spain but he couldn't risk him' ~ *Bobby Robson (England's 1982 'B' team manager and coach)*

'When Cyrille made his Albion debut in 1977, his two shining dark legs were greased with 'oss liniment. They were like oak trees, muscular and solid, and I saw steam rising from his head and blowing from his mouth. He was like a bull ready to attack. There and then he became my idol – what a player' ~ *Roy Morley (ardent Baggies' supporter)*

Twenty Things You Might Not Know About Cyrille

He spoke French (*Patios*) up to the age of eight.

Cyrille lived on the Caribbean island of St Lucia for a year before moving to the UK.

Won swimming certificates at school in the 100m and 200m events.

He gained seven CSEs at school.

Passed his City of Guilds 'B' grade electricians' exams in July 1977.

Played cricket for Borough of Brent in London.

Supported Tottenham Hotspur as a youngster.

Played against Luther Blissett in a football match in a London park.

Appeared on TV before becoming a professional with Albion – in an advert for Kronenberg: 'We won the Cup' which was shot at Twickenham rugby ground featuring the Hayes football team.

His first house cost him £24,000.

His first car was a brown Austin Allegro, and he crashed it on a night out with the 'real' Three Degrees.

His daughter, Michelle, was named after the famous Beatles song.

An Arsenal scout was sacked after failing to spot Cyrille's potential.

Manchester City wanted to sign Cyrille before he joined West Brom.

In the post at WBA, he received a bullet, wrapped in a cotton wool pad, with a note attached saying, 'If you put your foot on our Wembley turf you'll get one of these through your knees.' Cyrille still has the bullet!

He lost £500 to the Brighton defender Steve Foster in a card game. He hasn't gambled since.

The death of Laurie Cunningham had a very profound effect on Cyrille who admitted, "LC was visually stunning – he had pace, grace and style. I could watch him all day."

He sung on England's 1982 World Cup record – 'This Time We'll get It Right' – but he didn't make the squad for Spain.

Cyrille had a steel wire inserted in his face after fracturing his cheek bone in a clash with the West Ham United defender Joe Gallagher in January 1983. He was admitted to Whitechapel hospital, London, and was out of action for six weeks, missing five League games.

In 1984, Albion Chairman Sir Bert Millichip doubted if Albion would get £600,000 for Cyrille. Soon afterwards, Baggies' manager Johnny Giles sold him to Coventry City for £250,000 + VAT.

In 1985, Coventry tried to sell Cyrille to Wolves for just £40,000.

In March 1993, Cyrille was on the verge of returning to West Bromwich Albion on loan from Aston Villa. But negotiations between the two respective managers, Ron Atkinson (Villa) and Ossie Ardiles, and Cyrille himself, broke down.

Cyrille had a bone growth on his thigh and this, seemingly, put Ron Atkinson off from signing him for Manchester United.

In the world of music, Marc Bolan and T-Rex, Bob Marley, James Brown, David Bowie, the Temptations and Augustus Pablo were his favourites. And oh, we can't forget the original Three Degrees!

And finally, I first met Cyrille in 1977 and had the pleasure of taking his son, Robert, for PE, games and art at Astwell Preparatory School in Birmingham for three years.

Bibliography

A list of publications I have referred to during my research for this book:

Cyrille Regis: My Story (with Chris Green, 2010, Andre Deutsch/ Carlton Publishing)

'Smokin' Joe': Cyrille Regis – 25 Years In Football (TM, 2002, Britespot)

West Bromwich Albion: The Complete Record (TM, 2012, DB Publishing))

Wolverhampton Wanderers: The Complete Record (TM, 2008, Breedon Books)

Aston Villa: The Complete Record (Rob Bishop & Frank Holt, 201, DB Publishing)

Coventry City: A Complete Record (Rod Dean, 1883-1991, Breedon Books Sport)

The Essential History of England (Andrew Mourant & Jack Rollin, 2002, Headline Publishing)

Rothmans/Sky Sports Football Year Books, 1978-1996 (Rothmans/ Headline Publications Ltd)

Samba in the Smethwick End (Dave Bowler & Jas Bains, 2000, Mainstream Publishing, Edinburgh)

Robbo – My Autobiography (Bryan Robson with Derick Allsop, 2006, Hodder & Stoughton)

The Three Degrees (Paul Rees, 2014, Constable, London)

'Celebration 1979: Tribute to Laurie Cunningham, Cyrille Regis & Brendon Batson' (Cornerstone Marketing Ltd)

West Bromwich Albion: The Atkinson Years (Glenn Willmore, 2004, Perspective Publishing)

West Brom's Cult Heroes (Simon Wright, 2006, Know The Score Books)

Wembley: The FA Cup Finals, 1923-2000 (Glen Isherwood, Britespot)

I have also thumbed through numerous newspapers, football magazines and matchday programmes as well as watching YouTube footage to clarify certain relevant statistics and events while compiling this book. There is some conflicting information in these sources and therefore I have made judgement as to which is likely to be correct.

*Laurie Cunningham, Cyrille Regis and Brendan
Batson, known as "the 3 degrees" by fans*

Cyrille in the colours of Chester City

Cyrille scored six goals on tour to China and Hong Kong in 1978

Cyrille in action for Wycombe

Cyrille celebrating for Wycombe Wanderers, 15 October 1994

*Cyrille heading for goal as a Coventry City
player, against Arsenal, 1985*

In action for Coventry City

Last appearance for
Wycombe, 6 May 1995

Cyrille in action for Hayes, 1976

*Tony presenting Cyrille Regis with his "Australian"
supporters' club player of the year award in 1979*

*Cyrille playing for Wycombe Wanderers, against
Birmingham City, 18 March 1995*

*Cyrille makes his debut for Wycombe Wanderers against
Cambridge, Wycombe won the game 3-0, 13 August 1994*

Cyrille running out of the tunnel ahead of Wycombe's FA Cup tie against West Ham United, 7 January 1995

Cyrille grabs a late equaliser for Wycombe with a close range header against Plymouth, 15 October 1994

Cyrille in action for Wycombe, against Stockport County, 4 March 1995

*Cyrille in action for Wycombe, against Brighton
& Hove Albion, 26 December 1994*

*Cyrille shows his ability in the air during his final appearance
for Wycombe, against Leyton Orient, 6 May 1995*

Cyrille shields the ball from West Ham's Alvin Martin whilst playing for Wycombe in the FA Cup 3rd round, 7 January 1995

Cyrille showing his Chester colours

Cyrille taking to the field to start his debut for Coventry against Newcastle, October 1984

Cyrille in action for Wycombe, against Cambridge, 13 August 1994

Cyrille at Buckingham Palace with his MBE

Promotional card, drawing by artist Bob Bond
(reproduced with kind permission by Bob)

Cyrille with his children Robert and Michelle